SACRED MOUNTAINS

How the revival of Daoism is
turning China's ecological
crisis around

Sacred Mountains

First published in 2014 by
Bene Factum Publishing Ltd
PO Box 58122
London
SW8 5WZ

Email: inquiries@bene-factum.co.uk
www.bene-factum.co.uk

ISBN: 978-1-909657-56-4
Text © Allerd Stikker
Illustrations © Rosa Vitalie

A CIP catalogue record of this is available from the British Library.

Cover and book design by Rosa Vitalie
Printed and bound in Slovenia on behalf of Latitude Press

Picture credits: All photographs are from the ARC archives or the personal collections of the Stikker family, Michael Shackleton and Lani van Petten.

MIX
Paper from
responsible sources
FSC® C110418

Allerd Stikker

SACRED MOUNTAINS

How the revival of Daoism is
turning China's ecological
crisis around

Editor Maja Nijessen

Design and illustrations Rosa Vitalie

Bene Factum Publishing

Contents

Foreword

In classical China, there was a model for the life of a powerful, successful man. He would start as a Confucian scholar, working tirelessly to become a master of his art. From this, he would progress through the hierarchy of power, rising ever higher and taking on more and more responsibility. Hard, tough decisions would be his to make. Then, at a certain point all this would cease to matter. There would come a time when the pen of authority was laid aside and the pen of poetry and reflection would take its place. Often, this involved a shift from the worldly view of the Confucian bureaucrat to the metaphysical, spiritual world of Daoism.

The journey of Allerd Stikker is in a way an example of this ancient Chinese way of living. But Allerd has brought a Protestant Dutch dimension to the story. His move from power and authority to the world of reflection inspired by Daoism did not mean a disengagement from the material world. Instead, he has brought these worlds together in a most extraordinary way. His journey along the Path of the Dao has taken him from ridicule in Taiwan in the late 1980s, when he first suggested that Daoism might be relevant to the crises of ecology, to the status of a leading personality in the Daoist world in modern China.

The reason? He saw that deep within Daoism lay insights, wisdom and a way of life which held the seeds for an alternative future, not just for China but for the world. He saw that the ecological crises that have come upon us all could be tackled using the best of modern science and the deepest of the ancient wisdom of China. So he set off with only the vaguest sense of where this might go but with a doggedness and a sense of optimism which has fuelled not just him but all those who have worked with him.

Firstly, through founding the Ecological Management Foundation (EMF), he sought to bring the world of commerce and business together with the world of the environmental movement. Not an easy task. Many people in the environmental movement work on rather simplistic models of good guys and bad guys, and business—especially big business—was definitely classified as the bad guys. But Allerd has helped break through such divisions.

Next, he sought to bring the worlds of Chinese tradition, especially Daoism, into alliance with the worlds of science and the environmental movement. A tougher path but one for which he found an ally in the Alliance of Religions and Conservation (ARC) and especially in me, as not just head of ARC but also as a China scholar.

It has been my delight to work with Allerd for a decade as (often literally) side by side we have watched the Daoist leaders and thinkers of today delve deep into their teachings and begin to apply their insights to tackling the huge crises that face China's ecology. We have seen the Chinese government move from initial doubt to the situation now where they see the Daoists as among their strongest allies in the struggle to convince the people of China to protect nature. We have helped the Daoists build eco-temples. We have assisted in the founding of new Daoist and Confucian movements dedicated to protecting nature and the people. We have helped as declaration after declaration has sharpened the Daoists' vision of the role they can play in building a conservation ethos across China.

Without Allerd, ARC could never have achieved a fraction of what this book will tell you about the developments in China. Without his friendship, neither I nor my colleagues could have been able to help the Daoists rise to be one of the greatest environmental champions of China.

Thank you, Allerd. This is your story, of which we are honoured to have been part. And the story you have started has only just begun...

Martin Palmer
Secretary General of the Alliance of Religions and Conservation (ARC)

Introduction

A journey of 1,000 miles begins beneath one's feet. The words of Chinese philosopher Lao Zi perfectly capture my wonderful journey through the world of Daoism over the past thirty years. What began as a casual acquaintance with Daoism on the island of Taiwan, which I visited on many business trips in the 1980s, has led to a close partnership with the China programme of the Alliance of Religions and Conservation (ARC), a British non-governmental organisation that since 1995 has collaborated with the world's faiths to protect nature and create ecological awareness.

On the way, I discovered how the Daoists' cosmological view of the world, where humanity and nature are inextricably linked, fits in beautifully with my personal ambition to achieve a better global balance between economy and ecology. And I also discovered how well this ambition dovetailed with the mission pursued by ARC.

It's been a privilege to work with ARC and together contribute to the restoration of a Daoist temple in China and the development of the Daoist Ecology Temple Alliance. It's been fascinating to see how these achievements have given the Daoists some room for manoeuvre in Chinese society and how Daoism is even openly cited by the political establishment as the answer to the immense ecological and social problems facing modern China. And it's all the more amazing when you realise that the country is officially atheist with absolute rulers who, in the past century, have tried their very best to wipe Daoism off the map as a 'backward superstition'.

But the cultural and spiritual tradition of Daoism has withstood the storms of history. It has proven to be just as solid and unyielding as the rocks of the sacred mountains, a traditional Daoist symbol of the link between heaven, earth and humanity since time immemorial. These mountains have become a source of inspiration for my journey, for ARC's journey, for the future of China and for the harmony between ecology and economy worldwide.

We have not yet reached our final destination, but every step towards the top of the mountain is another step closer and the views along the way are simply breathtaking.

Allerd Stikker
January 2014, Bonaire

The Dao exists, Dao is

but where it comes from I do not know.

It has been shaping things,

From before the First Being,

From the before the Beginning of Time.

Chapter 4 of the Dao De Jing

1

A Journey into Daoism

A Personal Story

Is there such a thing as a beginning or does everything flow from something else, from something that happened earlier? This is not just a philosophical thought but a practical dilemma I ran into when I embarked on this book. How should I begin a story that lies so close to my heart? How should I describe my introduction to a world view that goes back to well before the modern calendar and yet fits in seamlessly with my outlook on life 2,500 years later? How should I relate the incredible journey I was fortunate enough to share with the Alliance of Religions and Conservation (ARC), a journey that has not only awakened ecological awareness in China but also contributed to the restoration of Daoism right at the core of Chinese society? Does it begin in Taiwan, where I first encountered Daoism over thirty years ago? Or does it begin with the tragic loss of Daoism in China in the last century, culminating in the complete destruction during the Cultural Revolution of all that smacked of religion? Or does it begin with the establishment of ARC, a passionate British NGO that countered conventional wisdom and showed the world how religion and nature conservation can form an effective partnership for the care of our planet?

With none in particular and with all simultaneously, I concluded. The stories run concurrently and converge or intersect somewhere in my tale. My dilemma illustrates why we should move away from a strict adherence to the linear concept of time familiar to us in the

West. In good Daoist tradition, we should view time as relative and experience it whenever the story calls for it.

To keep things simple, let's take my business trips to Taiwan at the end of the 1970s as our point of departure. In that period, I was at the helm of RSV, a large Dutch shipbuilding company that produced naval equipment, and I travelled around the world to secure new orders. This also took me to Taiwan. Negotiations there always required patience and frequent meetings at the highest ministerial and military levels. They could easily be thwarted by more urgent government meetings and various other affairs and would then be postponed. This may have been inconvenient on some occasions but the unexpected gaps in my schedule gave me the opportunity to get to know the country, its people and its culture a little better. So I spoke to my negotiation counterparts about their daily lives, I asked around for tips about sights worth visiting, I often went out exploring and spent many hours reading in my hotel room or in the lobby. I relished being away from the rough and tumble of hectic meetings and being able to experience for a moment the perspective of local everyday life.

Taiwan opened my eyes in more than one way. At that time, the country was known as the Economic Miracle of the Far East. But I felt it was turning into the Ecological Disaster of the Far East: the impressive double-digit economic growth appeared to have a dark downside. At certain times, the streets of Taiwan were blanketed in a thick cloud of smog that had the millions of inhabitants reach for their face masks. The myriad cars and scooters that snarled up the roads during rush hour relentlessly spewed exhaust fumes into the air. The northern suburbs of the city, in particular, showed a skyline silhouette of large-scale industry, a very likely contributor to the pollution of air, soil and water. In the absence of a proper sewerage system, the many canals and rivers on the island were treated as *de facto* sewers, and not only by households. It gave the waterways in the city and far beyond an unsavoury look. I wasn't surprised to read at the time that Taiwan had the highest incidence of hepatitis patients in the industrialised world.

I was shocked by the magnitude of the ecological disaster that appeared to be in the making here. But I was equally amazed by the matter-of-factness with which people seemed to put up with the situation. It was as if an unwritten law made environmental pollution some kind of inevitable, collateral damage of economic growth. I began to realise that ecology was a complete non-issue in the average Taiwanese boardroom and that this was in fact no different in Europe. The global paradigm of economic growth and a rising standard of living left little room for ecological considerations. And on this island, the consequences of such a denial were patently visible.

Somewhere, something had gone wrong. Surely, humankind, *Homo economicus*, did not mean to destroy the earth, a planet that had existed for billions of years and had reinvented itself time and again. Could it be that we, human beings, had lost sight of things? Were we allowing economic considerations to weigh too heavily vis-à-vis any concern for our habitat? Perhaps I wouldn't or couldn't quite accept that, as the CEO of a large company, I was myself part of the economic apparatus. But one thing's for sure: these thoughts planted the first seeds that grew into my subsequent outlook on life.

Taiwan was also the very place where I became acquainted with the more than 2,000-year-old tradition of Daoism, a view of the world where the link with nature plays a pivotal role and a view that I would come to cherish. My negotiation counterparts were highly educated Taiwanese people, many having attended the prestigious United States Naval Academy, where they had been tried and tested. And yet they had remained firmly rooted in their own Taiwanese culture, which still had close links with Daoist tradition, as it turned out. I was very surprised to observe that, apart from a rational side, they also had a more intuitive approach to life. They told me, for instance, that in Taiwan palm-reading is generally considered an appropriate way of determining an individual's well-being and providing medical advice. It seemed an amazingly simple way of monitoring and promoting people's health. My interest was aroused and I immediately suggested that they should look at my own hand. This was not as easy as I thought. An integral part of the ritual was that I should first join them for dinner one evening, so they could evaluate my constitution and movements properly. No sooner said than done: I spent an agreeable evening at the dinner table and the next day, to my surprise, was given a detailed analysis of my physical and mental health in the past, present and future. My hand told them that I was in good health but that I would have to be particularly careful between the ages of sixty-eight and seventy-eight. Furthermore, the first half of the 1980s would be a difficult period for me, after which my life would follow a completely different but happier path. I have to confess that, little by little, I came to realise that their predictions were surprisingly close to the truth.

I learnt subsequently that the palm-reading ritual was part and parcel of the Daoist tradition that still flowed through the veins of these officers despite their many years in the West. There was a bond with Daoism up to the highest levels. During the negotiations, I met General Wego Chiang, one of Chiang Kai-shek's two sons. Wego Chiang had also completed an education and military training in the West and was the author of many books on military strategy. More surprising was that, in 1981, he also wrote a book called *Dao and Human Nature* on Daoism. In one of our meetings, he gave me a copy of the book, complete with a personal message, as a present.

These very same officers put me onto the Long Shan Temple, a massive and colourful temple complex right in the busy centre of Taipei. The Cultural Revolution may have destroyed the cultural and religious heritage of mainland China, but had spared Taiwan. Its religious buildings and practices were still intact. When the officers told me about the Long Shan Temple, I didn't have the faintest inkling that here I would make a life-changing acquaintance.

On my way to the temple, I wandered between the blocks of flats, as dull as the many others I had seen in this huge city. And all of a sudden, a colourful, richly decorated entrance appeared out of thin air like a boundary between the drab asphalt of the busy road that ran alongside the temple and, on the other side, a courtyard resembling a kind of market. It appeared to be thriving with tiny stalls selling religious paraphernalia, incense sticks and traditional Chinese medicine. The square was crowded with people. I saw many Asians though very few Westerners. Just momentarily, I felt part of the personal lives of the local population, for whom this place played a key role—so I was told. I had read that the temple was built in 1738 by Chinese immigrants as a copy and remembrance of a Buddhist temple in Fujian province, their homeland. The original complex was rebuilt and renovated many times as a result of natural catastrophes and wars and, over time, the original Buddhist design was supplemented with references to Daoism and folk religions. Religious division and discord seemed to be a non-issue here.

In 1919, the complex was given its current form by Wang Shi Yuan, a famous architect from Fujian and, in his day, a master of traditional Chinese temple design. Since that time, the temple has come to be regarded as one of the finest specimens of traditional Chinese temple architecture. One look at the gate and main hall opposite was sufficient confirmation. The beautifully painted wood and stone engravings and the statues adorning the roofs and walls each told its own story in the minutest detail. From the rooftops, the carved wood dragons kept a close eye on the neighbourhood. This was a reference to Long Shan or Dragon Mountain, the name of the temple. It suddenly dawned on me that I had been negotiating about submarines in the so-called Sea Dragon Class the entire time, that I had invariably stayed in the Dragon Wing of the Grand Hotel, where I was a regular, and that my Chinese zodiac sign is the Dragon. Coincidence or omen? I entered the main hall and my attention was caught by an immense, golden statue. There, standing right before me, was Guan Yin! Her eyes were closed, her smile friendly yet mysterious, the envy of Mona Lisa, and her soft face completely overlaid with gold—I was riveted! And I wasn't the only one because people all around me showed their devotion in a multitude of ways, almost in a trance. Among the sometimes ferocious-looking gods I had seen here and elsewhere, she was a welcome relief. Such ineffable and timeless beauty. Was it love at first sight?

The Long Shan Temple was specially dedicated to her—it certainly explained her prominence in the main hall. In the course of time, all sorts of other gods had gathered around her, particularly from the temples in the areas that had been demolished as part of the city's sweeping development plans. The statues found at least temporary accommodation in Long Shan. And Guan Yin clearly felt at home. Even a bombardment by the US Air Force in 1945 had not dislodged her. Among the smoking remains of the temple, she had been the only one still proudly standing. When I got to know her better, I discovered that she had once been the male Buddhist *bodhisattva* Avalokitesvara and had crossed China's northern border. In the course of his mythical existence, he metamorphosed into the female Daoist deity Guan Yin. She is the goddess of compassion who hears all the sounds of the world. And she is the goddess who, since the day I first saw her, has accompanied me on the path of my life, whispering to me in many guises.

Meeting Guan Yin aroused my interest in Daoism. Whenever I had time, I read as much as I could about this view of life, acquired translations of the Dao De Jing and Zhuang Zi, and tried to immerse myself in the sometimes incomprehensible verses. The metaphors and parables teach you new things time and time again and their meaning seems to lie *between* more than *in* the lines. For a trained scientist like myself, it was a mystical literary-cum-philosophical experience. I had a degree in chemical engineering from Delft University of Technology in the Netherlands and a flourishing career in the chemical industry but had never been able to shake a nagging feeling that something wasn't quite right with Western science. It had taught me that the world is measurable and makeable and that scientific progress is making that world increasingly tangible and intelligible. But if this was the case, then why did I, as a student, have to plod my way through complex formulae and ingredients to create a particular dye, while nature allowed the plant in my student room to grow a beautiful red flower simply with sunlight, soil, air and water—no controlled laboratory conditions, no carefully selected substances and no bulky manuals. Somewhere, nature had access to processes of change whose origins were incomprehensible to us, the human race, notwithstanding all our scientific wisdom. The best we could do was to produce an unnatural copy of nature. Somehow, a yawning gap separated the scientific world of theoretical models and the real world of unpredictability. This gap had always intrigued me and made me conjecture that there was more between heaven and earth than what our ingenuity could only achieve imperfectly.

The gap between science and reality didn't stop us, rational beings, from exercising control over the world. From chemical processes that produced life-saving medicines to physical processes that allowed us to convert matter into energy—together these inventions laid a fertile foundation for an age of incredibly rapid and major industrialisation. In the short term, it clearly brought us higher standards of living in the West; but in the long term, the large-scale manipulation of transformation processes was starting to take its toll. Despite its enormous resilience, nature could barely keep up with the exponential increase in our consumption and pollution of natural resources. We were well on our way to making our planet, our own habitat, unliveable. I had seen, smelt and felt the unmistakable signs in Taiwan.

It led me to wonder about the human role in the transformation processes that drive evolution. Or for the more philosophically inclined: how did we arrive on earth and why—two basic questions about life that, at unguarded moments, invade our thoughts. In my own case, perhaps because of an innate desire to seek and find connections, such questions always lingered at the back of my mind.

The picture that gradually emerged from all the books and Daoist texts fit in perfectly with the answers I had formulated for myself over the years. I saw my own intuition articulated in the Daoist notion of the Dao, a source and driving force giving rise to everything—to life, the earth and the universe—and where everything returns. As if to challenge the knowledge I had assimilated throughout a lifetime, I had somehow always wondered about the overwhelming beauty, power and complexity of the earth and all that flowers and flourishes. Not having any definite scientific answers, I had concluded that everything originates from an ingenious pattern. There was no religious conviction in this belief as I had never felt comfortable with explanations based on an omniscient Creator responsible for the story of Creation. But it was very close to the Dao. This notion, moreover, encompasses unity and the interrelation between the universe, the earth and man as well as between the material and non-material worlds. What an eye-opener for the Western world, where mind and matter were treated as distinct and the human race had done all it could to wean itself from its environment.

On my journey through the Daoist mindscape, my own notions and ideas kept staring back at me. What's more, somewhere between the lines, I was beginning to suspect a link between this centuries-old Chinese cosmological view of the world and the world view of Teilhard de Chardin, a French Jesuit priest and palaeontologist who had lived in China—of all places—from 1923 until 1946 (on and off) and contributed to the research on *Homo pekinensis* or Peking Man. I had come across his work in 1963, when my mother gave me a copy of *Le Phénomène humain* (The Phenomenon of Man). The book was utterly amazing, taking me by complete surprise with its insight into the interdependence in the world around me. It gives a glimpse of Teilhard's search for an evolutionary theory that does justice to his scientific as well as Christian convictions. We see him build solid bridges between scientific, religious, social and mystical beliefs—a clever piece of creative and critical thinking, though it was not appreciated by the Catholic Church at the time. The book carefully maps the scientific knowledge available in Teilhard's day about the emergence of the universe, life on earth and the phenomenon of man. With my science background, I had great admiration for his solid scientific approach. Teilhard then shows that the evolutionary process advances in leaps and bounds according to a certain pattern. Substances and life forms develop into increasingly complex combinations with a growing level of consciousness, until they reach saturation as it were. At this point, the process jumps to a new model of growth with new forms of still greater complexity, though nobody can explain how it works even today. The earth thus came into being as an inanimate planet (the inorganic geosphere). At some stage, life originated as a sudden, one-off event (the organic biosphere). And then, in the relatively recent history of our planet and seemingly from nowhere, self-reflective consciousness emerged in the human race, or *Homo sapiens* (the cultural or spiritual noosphere).

Here, Teilhard indirectly expresses the doubts and questions I had always had about a purely scientific approach to the world around us. We may be perfectly capable of using conventional science to capture observable phenomena in positive and normative models. But they don't help us explain at the most fundamental level why these phenomena exist. Why did the universe, life, the human race and our self-reflective consciousness emerge? Our current scientific models focus exclusively on what is measurable and they compartmentalise our observations so that we lose sight of the unified whole. Teilhard gives these gaps in our knowledge meaning in his conclusion that the evolutionary process has an unmistakable pattern, direction and purpose, and leads to advancement whenever the process jumps to a more complex model. This process seems to be the result of non-material energy, a universal consciousness that can be traced back to all phenomena, of both mind and matter. Furthermore, the evolutionary process is not a static given but the outcome of a dynamic, creative interaction and connectedness between its constituent elements. The apex is the human race, the most complex organism: human beings with a self-reflective consciousness and the ability to transform their own micro world and thereby the macro world as well. In Teilhard's view, this self-reflective consciousness of humankind, and creation along with it, moves irrevocably towards the 'Omega Point', the maximum degree of consciousness and complexity where human self-reflective consciousness is absorbed into an ultimate divine unity. Teilhard believed human beings had the capacity and responsibility to look after their environment, the unity to which they all belonged. And although I didn't share Teilhard's Christian interpretation of the Omega Point, I thought his ideas helped underpin my own observation that humanity had the ingenuity—though not unlimited—to influence and steer transformation processes. As far as I was concerned, humanity had used this capacity in an unbridled and one-sided fashion, causing long-term harm to the environment. It was now time to sit up and redirect our ingenuity. We needed to mend what had been damaged through the ages.

I read Teilhard's book in one sitting and it has been etched on my mind ever since. And as I continued reading about Daoism, I began to sense that there were parallels between Teilhard and Dao and that these ways of thinking might well answer the unsettling questions I still had about the Western approach to science. A different question that kept running through my mind was why Teilhard's works didn't display any link with the Daoist view of life he had seen around him in China all those years.

It would take several more years before I had the time and space to weigh this question more carefully—until 1983 to be precise. This was the year the shipbuilding company I headed collapsed, dragging me down with it. The company was established in 1972, when political and trade union pressure led to a merger of the main shipbuilding companies in the Netherlands. The merger provided jobs for some 15,000 people and was expected to weather the growing foreign competition from countries like Korea and Japan, thereby safeguarding the future of Dutch workmanship. The merger was created with financial support from the state and was based on a new, comprehensive model of employee participation. One outcome of the democratisation process was a central works council consisting of twenty-two representatives of the participating companies. In 1973, I was invited to manage this challenging megamerger, catapulted from the board of what was then Dutch chemical company AKZO.

Reflections on Guan Yin

Guan Shi Yin, the goddess of compassion, who I met in Taiwan in the early 1980s and who has been with me ever since, has shown many faces in the long course of her enigmatic presence.

Many Western scholars believe that *she* started as *he* in the form of the male Hindu deity of compassion, or Avalokitesvara in Sanskrit, well before the Common Era. In the 1st century CE, Avalokitesvara gradually entered Indian Buddhism as a *bodhisattva*, as a being who, out of compassion, wishes to reach enlightenment, not just for himself but for the benefit of all sentient beings. Avalokitesvara was seen as the embodiment of infinite compassion: he vowed to postpone his own enlightenment until he had helped all sentient beings realise buddhahood. It was this *bodhisattva* who won the hearts and souls of the Chinese people when Mahayana Buddhism entered north-west China around 25–220 CE during the second (or Eastern) Han Dynasty. One of the central texts in Mahayana Buddhism, the *Saddharma Pundarika Sutra* or 'White Lotus Sutra', describes the works and ways of Avalokitesvara and was translated into Chinese at the beginning of the 3rd century CE. The name Avalokitesvara thus became its Chinese equivalent: Guan Shi Yin. During the Tang Dynasty, under Emperor Taizong (626–649 CE), Shi was dropped from his name in order not to offend the emperor whose personal name had been Li Shi Ming. Other sources say that Shi, which is generally translated as 'the world', belonged to the jurisdiction of the emperor and this word should not be used by the common people. After the Tang Dynasty (618–907 CE), Guan Yin was gradually depicted as a female deity in images, statues and prints. It was not uncommon for Buddhist deities to incorporate elements of Chinese belief and folk tradition as they entered Chinese territory, but none of them underwent such a profound transformation as Guan Yin. In 1119 CE, she was conferred the title of Daoist Goddess Cihang Pudu Yuantong Zizai by Emperor Huizong. Nowadays, she is revered by both Daoists and Chinese Buddhists as Guan Yin, the goddess of compassion.

Bit by bit, I am beginning to understand that this process of gender transformation stemmed from a need and desire for feminine compassion in a world of male-oriented Confucianism, ritual, hierarchy, power and fear. It was a need that seemed universal, leading not only to Guan Yin in Asia but also to the mythology of Isis in Egypt and Mary in Europe. China had not been entirely without a female deity: there was the Queen Mother of the West, a goddess rooted in shamanic culture. She had survived the Confucian removal of shamanic and feminine traditions and is still an important deity today. But she was distant and stern and did not fulfil the role of a compassionate goddess. Chinese cultural history lacked an element of genuine compassion until Guan Yin entered the Daoist pantheon.

So how does an ordinary Dutch businessman, who visited Taiwan in the early 1980s and knew nothing about Buddhism and Daoism, become spellbound and inspired by such a mysterious symbolic figure for the rest of his life? The answer is not easy, but a better understanding of who she is might shed some light on my fascination for her. I say *her*, because that is what she is to me: a woman of compassion, who connects with humanity in ways we often deny or are unaware of in our busy daily lives.

What attracts me in Guan Yin is that she is not a historic person, but a mythical *bodhisattva*, as described in the *White Lotus Sutra*. The *Lotus Sutra*, as it is generally known, depicts how Avalokitesvara arose from a light ray exiting the right eye of the Buddha Amitabha, as a symbolic messenger from beyond the material world, enlightened and pure. The name of the sutra is derived from the white lotus flower that emerges unstained and white from a muddy pool, as a symbol of purity and integrity arising from a messy world. Lotus flowers may come in many different colours but the lotus in the *Lotus Sutra* always stands for the white lotus. This symbolism is essential to the text.

The name Guan Shi Yin can be interpreted in different ways in both Sanskrit and Chinese and we cannot easily translate the words and symbols into our Western languages. Judging from a variety of translations, scholars agree on the following meaning: Guan represents 'see/hear from all around', Shi is the word for 'world' and Yin means 'sounds/cries/noises'. In my own interpretation, her name refers to 'she who listens to the sounds of the world'. And by sounds I mean happy as well as sad sounds. This is very much my personal perception because in the vast literature about her, including the old scriptures, the emphasis is on listening to people who are suffering, who are being threatened and who are in great need of help and hope. In Chapter 25 of the *White Lotus Sutra*, there is an extensive description of thirteen kinds of critical circumstances where Avalokitesvara will assist in solving your problems. Although ultimately, you will have to solve them yourself, he guides you through the process. The sutra then goes on to say that he can appear in your life in thirty-three different embodiments, depending on the kind of advice you need, on the moment he hears you and on the time you are receptive to his presence. He may appear as a male or female, as someone from a whole range of professions and even as an animal. Here, Avalokitesvara (or Guan Yin) is certainly a saviour of people in need. But I think Guan Yin hears and whispers sounds more generally. She is a companion who shares special moments in people's lives, guiding and inspiring those who listen to her. This symbolism has worked miracles in the last thirty years of my own life, consciously and sometimes unconsciously, but always with an awareness of her presence.

Since 1200 CE, Guan Yin has been exclusively depicted as female in art and literature. But when you look closely at her statues, imprints or paintings, it is clear that she has no female breasts—that there is in fact an element of androgyny. Perhaps this was how artists, who played a considerable role in the transformation process to a female goddess, were expressing the natural balance between male and female in Daoist cosmology. The transformation to a female deity coincided with the emerging Mary devotion in Europe and the arrival of the Christian Nestorian Churches in China. It is even speculated that the similarity

in statues and images of Mary and Guan Yin has been the result of mutual influence. Whether or not there is a link, I think Guan Yin is a very different deity, without a human history and with a universal presence, not linked to any single religion, and honoured and revered by lay people as well as non-religious people like myself. For me, she transcends all religions and world views: in her silence, she is accessible to all.

The story of Guan Yin is a complex and fascinating tale and I have merely outlined the essence here. To me, it is a story I needed to capture in order to understand why she is my inspiration in the search for a meaningful life. Scholars, scientists and other writers have produced numerous volumes on the history, evolution and universal dimension of the Guan Yin phenomenon and why she developed into a female goddess in China. I now understand there was a dormant—and perhaps universal and timeless—need and desire within Chinese Daoist-based culture to have a compassion-oriented female deity within a pantheon of stern and scary male deities.

When I was confronted with the overwhelming presence of Guan Yin for the first time, as she radiated in the Long Shan Temple in Taipei, such feelings penetrated my mind and soul. I knew nothing of all that I am writing now, but her silent presence, her elegant stance, her peaceful face and her obvious popularity impressed me very much. And from that day, I have never been without her. She has been listening to my sounds and I have been listening to hers. In the past thirty-odd years, this symbolic exchange of messages has worked wonders for me. They are not expressed in written or spoken words, nor are they measured or calculated. Guan Yin has opened my ears and eyes to what I did not see before. She is my connection with the meta world, a world beyond time and space, beyond eternity and infinity.

観音

Shortly after taking up my new position, the global recession set in, not only in the Netherlands but also in France, the United Kingdom and Sweden, where reputable shipyards felt the scourge of cut-throat competition from low-wage countries and the second oil crisis. It was clear that the new company was in dire need of major restructuring. But this was where the lack of organic unity and the artificial amalgamation of companies with different cultures, histories and rates of return started to backfire. Decisions were being hindered and discussions were never-ending. Meanwhile, the ship was starting to list dangerously. In 1979, my last attempt at fundamental change was rejected by the organisation, the political establishment and society at large. I then tendered my resignation, which was also rejected. The ship finally went down in 1983 and I had to step down. The loss-making activities of the company were shut down immediately while others continued independently in pared-down form.

As was to be expected, the downfall of the company caused a great deal of commotion. People often asked me afterwards if I wasn't shocked by the whole situation. But to be honest, it didn't take me by surprise because I had seen it coming for some four years. My primary concern was: what could be learnt from this experience? This practical response was undoubtedly driven by my practical outlook but perhaps just as much by a desire to avoid ever again being confronted by a situation of crisis where time and inertia were stuck in a deadlock. These lessons would manifest themselves over the years. Meanwhile, I had discovered the accuracy of the Chinese characters for 'crisis', symbols which can roughly be translated as 'threat' as well as 'opportunity'. This was indeed my own experience. I moved to London to put some distance between myself and the whole situation and to create some peace and quiet so I could explore the connection between the world views of Teilhard de Chardin and Daoism. The crisis had offered me the opportunity to venture along completely new paths and gain new insights. Besides, I saw the past as something we should learn from rather than suffer for. The lessons from my RSV period would form a crucial compass that guided me on every journey I undertook subsequently, something I gradually came to understand from my research into Teilhard and Daoism.

Not long after my resignation, the RSV receiver asked me to go to Taiwan so I could explain to our clients what had happened. These were tough talks, to put it mildly. I had to announce the downfall of RSV after all. I was however able to tell them that the submarines would be completed and delivered, as would indeed happen in 1985. But what I remembered mostly was the cordiality and respect with which ministers and officers continued to treat me. To my surprise, I was wined and dined on my birthday, which happened to fall in that week. What a difference from the Netherlands, where immediately after my resignation all fell silent around me. There, my 'outside', my position and status were lost. The officers in Taiwan seemed to look more to the 'inside': people first and then business.

After my introduction to Teilhard's ideas in 1963, I joined the British, American and French Teilhard Associations. At certain moments, I attended lectures about Teilhard whenever it could be combined with my business trips. One such occasion was in 1981, when the American Teilhard Association celebrated Teilhard's hundredth birthday with a large conference in Arizona and a lecture by the chairman of the association, Thomas Berry. This Catholic priest, cultural historian and eco-theologian was not only an authority on Teilhard but also on Buddhism and Daoism. He was, moreover, a lecturer in the history of religions at Fordham University in New York and had studied the language and culture of China extensively. At this point, several of the paths I had tentatively been setting out for myself were starting to converge. There were my negotiations in Taiwan, my acquaintance with Daoism and my first ideas about a link between Teilhard and Dao. In a quiet moment, I walked up to Berry and we began to exchange ideas. I was inspired and impressed by the knowledge of this amiable man and his distinguished appearance and resolved to visit him again to find out more about Teilhard. At one point, I told him that I suspected a link between Teilhard's views and the views of Daoism. This seemed the kind of hypothesis he would perhaps have considered himself. Far from it, however: Berry looked at me with enquiring eyes, interrupting for a moment what had been a lively conversation. No, he concluded, after some thought—any such link is too far-fetched and you don't want to go down that path. But I thought it was worth the effort at least to figure out whether and why there shouldn't be any link.

From 1983 onwards, I paid regular visits to Berry at his home in Riverdale on the outskirts of New York City, along the rolling east bank of the Hudson River. I'll never forget the many occasions sitting in his garden on a bench under an imposing, centuries-old oak tree, chatting and philosophising. The view of the famous Palisades on the other side of the Hudson no doubt inspired new views of our own. The 'oak-tree sessions' helped me enormously to sharpen my understanding of Teilhard's world view. Conversely, they must have given Berry new ideas because in one of the sessions he concluded that a link between Teilhard and Dao wasn't such a strange proposition after all and definitely deserved closer examination. Keep going in this direction, he encouraged me, and I'll help whenever I can.

In my search for a link, I could hardly avoid the questions of whether someone else might have made the connection between Dao and Teilhard and why Teilhard had not seen the parallels himself. The only answer I could find to the first question came in the form of a French Franciscan sister, Marie-Ina Bergeron, who was an avid devotee of Teilhard's ideas and had worked in China as a missionary for over twenty years. I paid a visit to a home for Sisters of Mary in Paris, where she was enjoying her retirement. Before me stood a small woman with fine features, looking surprisingly energetic and determined—a perfect reflection of her impressive life. Bergeron had travelled to China as a missionary in 1939 during the turbulent years of the Chinese Civil War. In the following decades, the Chinese Communist Party, victorious in 1949, unleashed a veritable witch hunt against all that reeked of capitalism, religion and bourgeoisie. Bergeron ended up in prison and didn't come out for over two years. As fate would have it, a fellow prisoner turned out to be a Daoist monk. Here she could exchange ideas as much as she wanted and get a first-hand reading of Daoism. In these bizarre circumstances, she began to see a link between the ideas of Teilhard, the visionary fellow believer she had actually known herself, and Daoism, the age-old view of the world that defined the country she had begun to identify with, in spite of and also because of her experiences. After her release and return to France, she devoted herself to China. She obtained a PhD in Sinology and, in 1976, wrote a book entitled *La Chine et Teilhard*, setting out what she had learnt in a Chinese prison. In this book, she focuses on the similarities between the cosmology of

Daoism and of Teilhard. Both see a continual interaction between two poles in the universe: material forces and immaterial forces. In Daoism, the poles are symbolised by yin and yang; in Teilhard's view, the poles are the energy of physics and the energy of the psyche, also known as radial energy and tangential energy. These opposite complementary poles are continually interchangeable, emanating from an eternal source (the Tai Chi in Daoism) and returning to that source (Teilhard's Omega Point). Everything that arises from or returns to that source— the material as well as the immaterial, man, humanity, earth and heaven—is inextricably connected in a continuous flux.

Bergeron might have been of old age in body but not in spirit. She was very interested and curious to hear my findings, visibly enjoying the exchange of ideas with a kindred spirit who, like herself, was captivated by Teilhard and Dao. She was still giving lectures for Teilhard Associations worldwide and had also taught at Fordham University, where Berry had a position. The two Teilhard scholars turned out to be acquainted.

Given his death in 1955, the people who had known Teilhard personally were of course few and far between. But in Paris I found someone else who had known him and very well indeed. This was Father Pierre Leroy SJ. Like Bergeron, he was enjoying his old age, in his case in an old people's home for Jesuit brothers in Paris. He had spent many years in Beijing, living in the same house where Teilhard in his days as a palaeontologist had also lived. In 1940, they had even worked together to set up the Institute for Geobiology, whose aim was to safeguard a library and a valuable collection of fossils for future research. The two gentlemen had shared ideas over breakfast every morning. Here was someone who might have the answer to a question that had consumed me since the start of my search: how could it be that, in the very heart of Daoist society, Teilhard had not seen a link between his own cosmological views and those of Daoism? The answer was simple: as palaeontologists and scientists, they had lived in an isolated world. Their work had been miles removed from the everyday life, let alone religion, of the wider community. Their Chinese colleagues, too, had severed the link with their Daoist roots. For this generation of young intellectuals, the world of science and progress didn't leave any room for anachronistic traditions. Teilhard had branded Daoism as world-denying, passive and non-innovative. As far as he was concerned, his conclusion that human individuals should take responsibility and actively work to make the world a better place stood diametrically opposed to the Daoist principle of wu-wei, or not going against the grain. With my knowledge of Daoism at that time, I could only conclude that Teilhard had indeed not really studied this Chinese view of the world.

My search also took me back to Taiwan. In one of my many conversations with scholars of Teilhard and Daoism, the name of Yves Raguin SJ had come up. This French Jesuit priest taught Daoist philosophy at the Catholic Fu Ren University in Taipei—to Chinese students but in English. He was moreover an authority on Teilhard and familiar not only with his ideas but also the person himself. Imagine my surprise when I first went to see him, the door swung open and I was welcomed by a tall, well-dressed man with strong features and friendly, enquiring eyes. This learned man was the spitting image of the Teilhard de Chardin I knew from pictures. Extremely well-read in Daoism, he wholeheartedly supported my search for parallels between Teilhard and Daoism. He even gave me a hand-written syllabus of his lectures on Daoism. I was touched by his genuine interest in the culture and religion of the country where he lived. He ardently championed 'enculturation' and felt that his fellow missionaries had the duty to do so as well and to look for ways of embedding Catholicism into the culture of their host country. A good piece of advice, I thought, that might have spared the world a great deal of grief.

That evening, back in my hotel room, I realised that it had all started here on this island: my introduction to Daoism, the vague notion that there might be a link between this view of the world and the views of Teilhard de Chardin, and finally my search for such a link. It had taken me to the remotest corners of my mind and of the world. I had arrived in a completely new world, where the sharing of ideas and insights was key and where everyone focused in their own way on the questions of how and why we occupied our place on earth and beyond. It was a world far removed from the familiar world of business and economics. Here there was room for fundamental, existential questions whose answers could not be measured in financial terms. And frankly, it was a welcome change to be received as an unknown, interested newcomer rather than a businessman. It was a world where I felt welcome and at home, a world that challenged me to examine my own Western ideas and modes of thought. And it was a world that invited me to put my findings on paper, the only way to organise my mind and come to a conclusion. It was the birth of *The Transformation Factor: Towards an Ecological Consciousness.*

I mapped the parallels and differences between the views of Teilhard and Daoism. What I found particularly striking was that these two traditions were separated by a gap of two thousand years, yet had arrived at more or less similar conclusions. Daoism had done so intuitively and Teilhard after a long struggle with Western scientific paradigms and a Catholic background. Both views of the world embrace the notion of unity and interconnectedness between universe, earth, man and nature. Inherent in this unity is also the inseparability of the material and the non-material, matter and mind, night and day, and all the opposites we regard as irreconcilable. The same unity also encompasses the notion that in evolution there is a pattern or a source where all that exists originates and returns and that is itself subject to the creative forces through which it arose. That source and the associated phenomena might be measurable in some cases but remain mysterious in others. By this time, the whole idea was as rational to me as it was revolutionary.

Equally, if not more, perplexing was how alien these conclusions were to the Western ways of thinking, which defined not only my own upbringing and education but that of the world's political and economic top. Western eyes remained closed to these ideas, notwithstanding that we were heading for a new shock or 'discontinuity'. The imminence of a new discontinuity was one of the conclusions I came to when I followed in Teilhard's footsteps and started looking for the most recent scientific knowledge about the origins of the universe and evolution. Based on many books, papers and lectures, I could only agree wholeheartedly with Teilhard's view that cosmological history is characterised by stepwise as well as gradual change. Science had not been able to explain the emergence of the universe, of life on earth and of self-reflective consciousness in the human race. Evolution kept reaching a new saturation point and then jumped to a new model. The same scientific studies had also taught me that we were on our way to the next saturation point in terms of evolution and the role there for humankind. The first worrying scenarios about the future of the earth and humanity appeared in 1972 in a report, *The Limits to Growth*, commissioned by the Club of Rome. The authors calculated that, if the exponential growth in world population, natural resource consumption, industrial output, food production and environmental pollution were to continue at the same rate without any policy change, we would be heading straight for a scenario of 'overshoot and collapse', the gloomiest scenario in the report. Future generations would inherit an unliveable planet, at least for humanity. The earth, after all, had proved its robustness in the course of evolution. Humanity would thus not only be a creator but also a casualty of its own ability to steer transformation processes.

I could see storm clouds gathering in the coming decades. And I had a strong sense of *déjà vu*: this potential megacrisis contained distinct elements of the European shipbuilding 'mini crisis' marking my RSV years. This was an important lesson from the past and I wanted to help prevent history from ever repeating itself. In this particular case, it meant helping the world avoid a global ecological macro collapse by persuading society to stop stalling and procrastinating. In fact, it had become clear to me that I wanted to devote the rest of my life to preventing such a scenario of collapse and to smoothing the ride to a new phase in evolution.

And this is precisely where Teilhard and Daoism could offer some answers. Compartmental thinking in radical opposites—the dominant tone in the West for many centuries—had seen its best days. The pigeon-hole mentality which we had relied on to organise our world—from science to business and from society to politics—might have been successful in terms of technological advancement and unprecedented growth in Western welfare, but in the long run was jeopardising that very same success. In the radical opposition created between ecology and economy, ecology had played second fiddle for too long.

This naturally led to the question of how we could achieve a proper balance before it was too late. In my opinion, a new equilibrium would be based on a new awareness of unity and coherence that didn't revolve around humanity but around the environment, of which humanity is an inseparable part. The human race would be aware of its place and role in evolution. With that awareness, we would be able to see the interdependence between economy and ecology and restore the balance. Elements of this new, holistic approach could already be seen in the natural sciences (quantum physics), psychology and environmental science.

Any shift in awareness would have to come from the bottom of society. A second lesson I had learnt from the collapse of the ship-building industry was that, in times of crisis, we can't expect solutions exclusively from extensive, global decision-making structures. The differences in culture, history and interests across participating countries simply get in the way of quick and effective decisions. Any solution would have to be a balanced interplay between top and bottom. A new, ecological awareness would have to grow within the individual, and spread organically to communities, companies, governments and ultimately to global structures. At the time, a promising example of this movement could be seen in the bioregions in the United States. There, individuals and companies had joined forces in largely self-sufficient communities that produced food and energy and processed waste in a sustainable fashion. This bioregional approach has inspired all kinds of local sustainable food and energy initiatives worldwide today. I saw a crucial role for media, educational and religious organisations in the dissemination of ecological principles. The new way of thinking would then reach all levels of society. Ultimately, international organisations would be pivotal in piloting Western societies worldwide from the industrial era to an ecological era. We did have to make haste if we didn't want to leave future generations with an uninhabitable planet within the next fifty years. But an initial outline of a new ecological awareness was clearly visible.

My research into Teilhard and Daoism had turned into a true journey of discovery and I spent many enjoyable evenings writing *The Transformation Factor*. In the process, I made sure to have my conclusions and interpretations continually examined by the scholars of Teilhard and Daoism I had met along the way. One was Ursula King, then lecturer in Comparative Religions at Leeds University. She was a prominent expert on Teilhard and focused on gender issues in world religions, including Daoism. She had responded enthusiastically to my idea of comparing Teilhard and Daoism, generously commenting on the chapters I sent her. She became so enthused by my project that, one day, she suggested I turn it into a thesis for an MA in theology. I was of course very honoured that my research and findings were worthy of a masters degree but, at the same time, had completely underestimated the amount of work it would require. For a proper scientific study, I had to cite all sources on every page with great care. It was a massive job but well worth doing because it had started to dawn on me that a Master of Arts degree would be a very apt complement to the Master of Science degree from my Delft past. With one foot in the world of science and the other in the world of the arts, I seemed to be able to unite in myself seemingly irreconcilable opposites in the academic world. I saw it as a modest, symbolic step towards creating a balance between complementary opposites that in the compartmental thought process of the West had been driven so far apart.

Inspired by this achievement and in a fit of exuberance, I decided to ask Joseph Needham, Chairman of the British Teilhard Association, to write a foreword to the book. I had spoken to him before as part of my research on the similarities between Dao and Teilhard. Needham's name had invariably cropped up in all the literature and in my conversations with other scholars of Daoism and Teilhard. He was a world-renowned authority on Chinese culture and science and had authored *Science and Civilisation in China*, an enormous multi-volume work. Daoism, moreover, was his special interest. At the time, I visited him at Gonville and Caius College in Cambridge, where he was Master. His office was a grand room in the best British university tradition, crammed with books he had collected on his many travels to China. He had immediately shown enthusiasm for my plan to explore the parallels between Daoism and Teilhard, and had supported me all he could with ideas and recommendations. Still, it seemed very unlikely that this busy, world-famous scientist would take the time and trouble to write a foreword to my book. I couldn't have been more wrong. He told me that he would consider my request and I received a hand-written foreword in less than a week.

I often look back at this chapter in my personal history and it still fills me with gratitude and amazement. In search of parallels between two divergent world views that seemed to have crossed my path quite spontaneously, I had become a passionate champion of global ecological awareness. How did this happen? How did a businessman educated in the sciences and a driving force of economic activity turn into an advocate of the green boardroom? And how did a Dutch atheist ultimately become bound up with a Daoist temple deep in the heart of China? I see the key as *serendipity*. In search of answers, I had been sidetracked by other worthy views and behaviours. Each contributed to what in hindsight might be seen as a perfectly logical story but, in the first instance, seemed to surface by chance. If you keep your eyes and ears open, life will throw unexpected opportunities in your path. It's an adage I've been only too aware of ever since my encounter with Guan Yin, the Daoist goddess who passes on the sounds of the world to me at certain moments. I sometimes feel that the serendipity in my life actually bears her name.

Daoism

Daoism, in its major forms, is a descendant of shamanism. It is China's only indigenous religion if you discount Confucianism as a religion. As such, it is little understood outside China because it has never, as a religion, sought to convert outside China, nor to have any role outside China until the last few decades. Yet one of its core books, the Dao De Jing, is amongst the most popular religious texts on sale in the West and its symbol of yin-yang has passed into Western culture to express a model of relationships which the West does not have or has not expressed so succinctly.

Daoism may have found its way throughout the whole world but its origins remain obscure because we simply don't have enough historical sources. The Dao De Jing itself doesn't give a date and Lao Zi, its putative author, is more likely to be a mythical than historical figure.

What we do know is that the most important texts, the Dao De Jing and the Zhuang Zi, date back to the 4th century BCE, to the time Confucian principles were starting to take root. The authors didn't consider themselves as religious leaders at all, but more as thinkers and philosophers, responding to the extraordinary outburst of religious and philosophical thought which blossomed in China from the 6th to 3rd centuries BCE— the so-called Hundred Schools era.

What we also know is that Daoism reflects the anti-Confucian values of the shamans: the Way of those who reject hierarchies and controls, who mock 'success' and power, who take to the mountains to meditate and who listen to the voices of the spirit world. It is the Way of the spontaneous, the humorous and the quixotic. This is wonderfully captured in the Zhuang Zi, a witty commentary on the Confucian focus on morality and order.

The link with shamanism is that Daoism sought to grapple with the essence of nature and its relationship to this material world and to the world of the spirits. It took the two material and spiritual worlds of shamanism and unified them through the overarching role of the Dao, beyond the moral force of Kong Fu Zi, to be the primal energy of the Origin of all beginnings. Dao is commonly translated as 'Way' or 'Path', but it has a much wider connotation. It is concisely described in Chapter 42 of the Dao De Jing, the heart of Daoism:

The Dao gives birth to the One,
the Origin.
The One, the Origin, gives birth
to the Two.
The Two give birth to the Three.
The Three give birth to every
living thing.

The two referred to here are yin and yang and the three are the Triad of Heaven, Earth and Humanity. At the same time, the Dao De Jing gives an early warning in Chapter 1 against trying to capture the Dao in words:

The Dao that can be talked about
is not the true Dao.
The name that can be named
is not the eternal Name.

Lao Zi

Lao Zi is possibly one of the most elusive of all religious founder figures. All that is recorded is that he was born sometime in the 6th century BCE, became the state archivist in the state of Chou and that he met Kong Fu Zi—as described by Zhuang Zi.

Legend doesn't provide much more. The heart of the Lao Zi story is not really his life but his departure from China, or indeed perhaps his death. It is said that Lao Zi despaired of the situation in China and packed his bags to leave. Heading west—the direction of enlightenment, just as the East is for Europe—he stopped for the night with the gatekeeper of the pass across the mountains to the West. The gatekeeper asked him to leave a message or guideline for

those left behind and legend tells us that Lao Zi wrote the Dao De Jing that night. Handing it over to the gatekeeper, he then departed west and was never seen again.

Daoism as Religion

The quest for personal salvation and meaning in China only began to surface in the 3rd century BCE. Prior to this, it would appear that life after death was considered less important than just being an ancestor, and only the ancestors of the rich and powerful—especially ruling families—were considered truly significant. The ritual actions of the emperors each year at the Temple of Heaven and the Temple of Earth symbolise the old model of the human relationship with Heaven. All that was required was for the ruling Son of Heaven to speak on behalf of all people to Heaven and to Earth and all would be well. Meaning and purpose were to be found in an individual's place within the hierarchy of society and within the communal life of the extended family or clan.

The unification of China in 220 BCE under the first true emperor, Qin Shi Huang Di, brought about the gradual collapse of local states and their cultures, and the suppression of local mythologies and beliefs. These sweeping changes were instigated by the Confucian scholars, keen to superimpose a coherent ideology at the scholarly and official level. The resulting dislocation of people from their own local cultures is perhaps one of the reasons for the growth of a desire to find meaning in new forms. Thus, in the early 2nd century CE, there emerged a new expression of religion, built upon the back of shamanism and drawing inspiration, imagery and eventually even gods from the philosophical writers of Daoism. The origins of this religious development lie in the province of Sichuan, the birthplace of Zhang Dao Ling, a remarkable man who was reputed to have mastered and understood the Dao De Jing by the age of seven. He retreated from ordinary life to a cave in the sacred mountain of Qing Cheng Shan in Sichuan, where he meditated and began to teach. There, during meditation, Lao Zi appeared to him and gave him the authority to organise religious communities, to forgive faults and sins, to heal and, most important of all, to exorcise ghosts, demons and evil spirits. Zhang organised the first full-scale religious expression of Daoism, and his Five Bushels movement, named after the entry fee of five bushels of rice, soon spread across Sichuan and into neighbouring provinces.

Daoist Movements

Over the next five hundred years, many different schools of Daoism arose focusing around revelations, healing, ritual, oracles, and shamanic practices. Together, they developed monasteries and nunneries and established a network of temples throughout southern China.

Nowadays, Daoism still comes in many different schools, of which the Zhengyi and the Quanzhen are the most prominent ones. The Celestial Masters' School (Zhengyi) is that of Zhang Dao Ling's descendants. Its main strength today lies in its network of 'parish priests' who minister to the faithful at the local level and who might be called upon to exorcise ghosts and demons, using the magic formulae of Zhang Dao Ling. The Quanzhen School only dates from the 12th century CE. It emphasises retreat from the world and hence has a strong monastic dimension. It also practises quite extreme forms of meditation and self-denial. One of its founding fathers, Wang Chong Yang, is reputed to have stood for two years in a hole in the ground, ten feet down, in order not to fall asleep.

Daoist Teachings

In practice, Daoism allows for many different forms and schools. But they all have the Daoist teachings as their starting point.

Daoism seeks to retain and maintain the balance between yin and yang, any pair of forces in the cosmos that are opposites and yet inextricably linked. Balancing yin and yang, Heaven and Earth, ensures the continuation of life itself. Through their rituals, Daoists act out the role humanity plays in this balancing act.

In order to do so, humanity needs to go with the flow, not fight against it—the principle of *wu-wei*. If you go

with the flow, you can achieve anything, but so much of human society is falsely constructed that this is
very hard. Here we see the shamanic
roots of Daoism. The worlds of material and spiritual must be kept in
balance and it is only by sublimating
the material world to the spiritual
that success can be achieved. But the
Daoists go beyond the shamans. The
Daoists believe that, through their liturgies, they can shape both the spirit
and material worlds. Indeed, they
believe that through the liturgies the
whole cosmos can be influenced as
long as this is done within the overall
flow of the Dao.

Daoist Ecology
Daoism has a natural relationship with
ecology. Kristofer Schipper, the widely
acclaimed sinologist and Daoist master, writes that in the early Common
Era the Daoists had already developed
institutions and rules whose role was
to protect nature and its natural balance. This was expressed in the '180
precepts' or guidelines for the leaders
of the lay communities in the early
days of Daoism. No fewer than twenty of these guidelines relate directly to
nature conservation and many others
do so indirectly. You could argue that
the Daoists are the pioneers of nature
conservation. In an entirely natural
way, they are the very first protectors
of nature. The Daoist Ecology Temple
Alliance and ARC have uncovered the
roots of Daoism and, with passion
and inspiration, have brought them
back to life.

The earth is a sacred vessel—

and it cannot be owned or improved.

If you try to possess it, you will destroy it:

If you try to hold on to it—you will lose it.

Chapter 29 of the Dao De Jing

2

The Price of a Miracle

The Ecology Issue on Taiwan

And there it was: *The Transformation Factor* on sale in Dutch bookshops in 1986 and in the English-speaking market from 1992. There was my name, in black and white, bound up with philosophy, religion and the environment. It was a world far removed from the micro- and macro-economic figures that had been my comfort zone until very recently. And what I discovered was that, in those days, economy and ecology were seen as poles apart. The environment and sustainability were non-issues in the companies and organisations where I had sat at the boardroom table. Even in the most favourable cases, they were subordinate to economic growth and were generally viewed as the domain of the back-to-nature brigade. I recall how the change in my perspective had elicited some frowns and sceptical looks from my former colleagues. It wouldn't surprise me if many thought I had gone cuckoo after the downfall of the shipbuilding company. But, I figured, the boardrooms were probably not yet ready for the ecological turnaround I felt was both necessary and inevitable. It may have appeared strange to the outside world but to me the new course was simply a logical consequence of my lifelong interests and experiences. And oddly enough, as the years go by, I see the interconnections more and more clearly. I now see and experience more clearly than ever the parallels between the process of evolution, the role of humanity in that process, and the challenges we are facing today.

Teilhard showed that evolution is punctuated by moments of saturation, moments which systems and organisms inevitably reach as they grow bigger, at which time new and more complex structures emerge. The degree of complexity in humans reached its apex when self-reflective consciousness emerged. The human race then stopped evolving— at least, the 'hardware' of the human body ceased to develop further. This wasn't true of our minds, which continued to evolve. Our intellectual capacity allowed us to go beyond the boundaries of our natural, organic ability. We extended our sight, for example, with the use of the telescope and our hearing through sound amplifiers. It led to a new way of thinking and structuring, to compartmental thinking— a catalyst for scientific and technological advancement. This was a mental world that enabled as well as demanded organisation. It was a world where the organic coherence of the evolutionary process was giving way to organisation as a key characteristic.

Something very similar is happening at the micro level of our body, a collection of cells that are perfectly capable of functioning organically and autonomously until something goes wrong and we resort to medicine. And what I came to see as a pattern also applied to RSV: shipbuilding companies that had grown organically were merged into a single organisation to help them cope with the economic crisis. In hindsight, the 'organised' had strayed too far from the 'organic': divisions were glued together without any attention to internal coherence and, when the crisis put pressure on the structure, the glue came unstuck and the company fell apart. Top-down organisation was no substitute for the coherence arising quite naturally from growth bottom-up. If anything, they were forces that had to be balanced.

The same phenomenon reared its head as a global ecological crisis at the macro level. Our organisational ability had given birth to consultative structures that were supposed to protect the environment worldwide. However, without any proper integration with the underlying organically grown social structures, the superimposed consultation procedures lacked force.

Organic versus organised: I was seeing more and more clearly the imbalance between these two opposites. It was another example of how our society was starting to disintegrate. Humanity excelled at organisation but we had begun to ignore our organic roots. And this is precisely what stood in the way of potential solutions to global environmental problems and the restoration of the balance between economy and ecology.

These were important lessons from my recent past and they pointed me in the direction of the solutions I describe in *The Transformation Factor*. And the beauty was that the human urge to organise I had derived from the Teilhardian model of evolution could also be found in Daoist writings, and in one of my favourite texts from the Dao De Jing, namely Chapter 18:

When the simplicity of the Dao's natural way erodes,
Virtue and honesty arise.
When these no longer suffice, intellect and wit set the tone,
And hypocrisy emerges.
When integrity is thus lost, rules and regulations take over,
Drawn up by wise men and civil servants.
And this is when chaos enters society.

Here we have poetry expressing the fatal organisational excesses which can arise when the balance between the organised and the organic is tipped to one side. The words are a pointed reference to the universal human craving for rules and structures in organisation and governance. And they show why the change in direction needed to safeguard the liveability of our planet cannot primarily come from global institutions.

It had become clear to me that the balance between economy and ecology could only be achieved through a complete turnaround in our ways of thinking, starting with the individual. Every one of us could become more aware of our own place and role in evolution, our role in a universe where coherence is key. We would then realise that our actions have an enormous impact on the environment and this in turn would lead to a more ecologically responsible mentality and behaviour. A renewed ecological awareness would then spread from individuals to communities and companies and then to countries and international organisations. The final outcome would be a world view, inspired by the religious and philosophical traditions of Daoism and Teilhard, that could reconcile the opposition between ecology and economy. Old wisdoms as a way out of modern problems—an inspirational thought, in my opinion.

This was my conclusion but of course the question was: what could I do myself to put it into practice? I was a practical person by nature and Delft University had only reinforced this. One of the most valuable legacies from my university days was that students were trained to look beyond theories. It was not enough for a chemical engineering student to develop a theoretical model; it also had to have practical relevance. This mentality always served me well during my working life. And now, it made me ask the inevitable question of what I could do myself to help create awareness and reintegrate ecology with economy.

The answer came from an unexpected quarter. In one of the oak-tree sessions, I shared my dilemma with Thomas Berry. I told him I was looking for a way to put the conclusions from my book into practice. He said he could basically see three ways to effect change. One was to climb the barricades for an all-out fight against the structures that required change. But I didn't exactly see myself as a revolutionary rebel. Another option was to effect change by working from within the system. But I had just left a busy career in business and was now travelling down a completely different path. I had closed the door on any return to the boardroom. Berry's third way was that of marginal action: challenging a system and stimulating change from the sidelines rather than from the epicentre. And that was it! I realised that this method was made for me. During my search for the similarities and differences between Dao and Teilhard, the unencumbered role of interested outsider had suited me very well. It had led to inspirational meetings and valuable insights. Marginal action would become a guiding principle for my endeavour to achieve and structure the balance between ecology and economy.

It was also Berry who reminded me of my own stories about the deplorable environmental situation in Taiwan. As we were discussing these things, we decided that the relatively isolated location and small size of this island, its spectacular economic growth and its measurable environmental problems made it a perfect candidate for a study on how to reintegrate economy and ecology. By way of comparison: Taiwan is exactly the same size as the Netherlands but, at the time, supported a population of 22 million people who occupied only a third of the total area in what was a relatively mountainous country. It occurred to me that, with this plan, I would come full circle. The island where I had started my search and where I had collected so many fond memories and experiences would receive the ultimate fruits of my journey. It was a good plan but I didn't have a clue how I should go about it.

It was again Berry who gave the first push when he put me onto Gerald O. Barney, a good friend of his. At the end of the 1970s, this physicist had directed *The Global 2000 Report to the President*, an international study on sustainability commissioned by US President Jimmy Carter. The report appeared in 1980 amid great public interest and was seen as a follow-up to the Club of Rome report, *The Limits to Growth*. The report outlined some inauspicious scenarios for the future based on figures, trends and the relationship between a growing world population, raw material consumption and environmental pollution. Berry knew they were working on regional versions of the report and suggested I talk to Barney about my idea for a study on the situation in Taiwan.

I visited Barney at his office in Washington and our meeting turned out to be the first step in a project whose size and impact I could not have foreseen at that time. This was to be the *Taiwan 2000 Report*. Barney welcomed my proposal wholeheartedly and we made a rough plan for the overall set-up and financing options. It was clear applications for project-funding and administration alone necessitated a formal organisation. So in 1984, I set up the US-based Trans-Form Foundation, the official birth of the *Taiwan 2000 Report* if we stretch the truth a little. This enabled us to start looking for funding and a suitable research design. The *Global 2000 Report* served as a perfect blueprint for the regional Taiwan report and gave us access to the most advanced models available at that time for generating future scenarios. One of the models used was the system dynamics methodology which Jay Forrester had developed at the Massachusetts Institute of Technology. This methodology made it possible, for the first time ever, to derive scenarios for the socio-economic future of the world based on a set of parameters and their interdependencies. The approach had been used previously in *The Limits to Growth*.

At the beginning of 1985, I wrapped up a research proposal and began to look for finance and to flesh out the project details. My first stop was Dr Sheldon Severinghaus, the then representative in Taiwan of the Asia Foundation. This US foundation, with which many Chinese immigrants in North America are affiliated, focuses among other things on sustainable and cultural development in Asia. Severinghaus lived in Taipei and I can still picture him in the bar of the Grand Hotel in that city, where I first met him. I laid out my plans and he instantly saw the potential. With his extensive knowledge and network in Taiwan, he was able to give the research a pivotal push in the right direction. His wife Lucia Liu was Professor of Zoology at National Taiwan University and, together with four colleagues from geography, sociology, economics and environmental engineering, was willing to serve on the Steering Committee, which would direct the project. This meant that the task of project implementation and project account-ability lay with National Taiwan University, in collaboration with Academia Sinica, another local academic institution. A local Taiwanese basis was a prerequisite for funding from the Asia Foundation and Rockefeller Brothers Fund, a sister organisation to the Rockefeller Foundation, one of whose tasks was to advance social change towards a more sustainable world. I was also able to recruit Philips Taiwan and Royal Dutch Airlines KLM as sponsors.

By this time, the project had unequivocally entered a new phase. The Steering Committee was now clearly in control and my role as an initiator was pushed further and further into the background. Every now and then, I looked with amazement at what had happened in such a short period and how the project was already moving forward inde-pendently and at full speed. I was kept informed of all developments but no more than that and, on several occasions, actually had to work hard to stay involved. The truth is I had quietly made myself redundant. What started as a desire to put flesh on the conclusions of my book had grown into an international project of genuine significance. And frankly, I preferred it this way: initiating a movement and then leaving it to run its own course. I thought it was a good example of Thomas Berry's marginal action.

At the same time, I was still actively involved in attracting additional funding and Western specialists. They would be able to share their analytical methods and experience in environmental policy-making with the Taiwanese researchers. That search put me in touch with the Taiwanese government, who of course were informed of the research. The first official response was not exactly favourable. It was clear the highest authorities on the island refused to have anything to do with the environment. If it didn't stimulate—or worse—if it impeded the impressive economic growth of the country, it was considered irrelevant. On top of this, ecology was seen as a left-wing (read: communist) subject. And given its troubled relationship with mainland China, the political establishment in Taiwan saw anything that smacked of communism as a potential threat to the political and social stability of the island. But as the research progressed and the *Taiwan 2000 Report* became more visible in terms of size and impact, the mood began to change. In the end, the Taiwanese government also wanted to play a part in funding and shaping the project. This was not only a real financial boost, but it meant that there was formal support for the project in government circles. And this was where any future scenarios, conclusions and recommendations would ultimately end up.

In 1989 came the presentation of the final outcome, the *Taiwan 2000 Report: Matching Economic Growth with Environmental Protection*. The Taiwanese government launched the report in grand style and no less a person than Mr K. T. Li, the very architect of the Economic Miracle, gave the opening speech. What better way to recognise the hard work of the past five years and the conclusions drawn. And to think that the message didn't exactly put the government in a favourable light. The various analyses painted a less-than-rosy picture of the environment in Taiwan. The lack of interest and direction in the areas of waste, the environment and urban planning—together with the rapidly rising demand for energy and the growing industrial and agricultural sectors—were guaranteed to seriously impair the liveability of the island. The costs of continuing down the same path would be enormous.

To turn the tide, the report argued, a radical change of direction in economic and environmental policy was needed. It recommended that the Taiwanese government should make haste to formulate, redefine and enforce environmental regulation. It would need a whole host of short- and long-term measures, ranging from emission reduction to recycling, and from tackling illegal manufacture to developing water and air quality standards. Moreover, the environment should become an integral part of economic policy. Every development and expansion of economic activity should be measured in terms of its potential effect on the environment. This also meant that the whole of society should be engaged in environmental issues. Education, the media and citizens'

initiatives required support and opportunities for collaboration. A structured follow-up study was needed to examine more closely any threat to liveability, the environment and health on the island and to quantify these as a basis for long-term policy. The report advised looking to other countries for expertise, experience, technology and methodology.

Well before the ink on the final report was dry, the research findings were starting to take effect. In the second half of the 1980s, an awakening ecological awareness took hold of Taiwan. For the first time ever, there was a popular outcry against the destruction of the everyday world. Violent protests by residents, for example, persuaded the US Dupont chemical company to abandon its plans to build a titanium dioxide plant near a coastal fishing village. The government too opened its eyes to the ecological crisis that threatened to swamp the country and, in 1987, it established a new ministry called the Environmental Protection Administration (EPA). In one fell swoop, environmental protection was promoted from a tiny office within the Ministry of the Interior with an annual budget of 5 million US dollars to a full-fledged, independent ministry with an annual budget of 1 billion dollars. I was pleased that two members of the Steering Committee also had positions in the EPA. The report was thus of immediate practical relevance. A salient detail is that Pieter Winsemius, a former Dutch minister for the environment and then partner at consultancy McKinsey, was appointed as an advisor during the establishment of the new ministry. He had contacted me for some background information on the *Taiwan 2000 Project*. We met just before his departure and talked about my experiences. He then left for Taiwan with the report in his hand luggage.

The *Taiwan 2000 Project* was also noticed in the Netherlands and by film-maker Philip Engelen. Engelen had approached me with the idea to turn the story into a documentary on the ecological consequences of unbridled economic growth, with Taiwan as one of the examples. I helped out on the research and wrote it down in a book bearing the same title as the three-part series that came out in 1988: *De prijs van een wonder* (The Price of a Miracle). While my book detailed the scientific background, Engelen created a probing picture of the price paid by the global environment for the growth in our welfare and of the alternative scenarios that could turn the tide. In the episode on Taiwan,

Engelen painted a vivid picture that I had come to know so well and that had culminated in the *Taiwan 2000 Report*. I could practically smell the foul river odours and the suffocating smog in Taipei through my television screen.

But Engelen added something else: he juxtaposed the tragic living conditions in Taiwan with the Daoist principles of purity and care for the earth I had also encountered there. It reminded me of something that had been pushed to the background by all the commotion surrounding the report. This island, where the opposition between economy and ecology had taken on extreme dimensions, was essentially the place that could resolve that very same opposition and achieve a better equilibrium. The solution was of course Daoism, whose principles were present throughout the island and focused on unity and coherence in the material and immaterial worlds around us.

I decided to weave this notion into a talk I had prepared for a final meeting on the *Taiwan 2000 Report*. Sheldon Severinghaus and Lucia Liu had invited all those involved to an informal evening at their home and had asked me, as the initiator, to say a few parting words. In the presence of some of the best and most promising Taiwanese scientists, all with degrees from top US universities, I outlined how my acquaintance with Daoism in Taiwan had ultimately led me to the *Taiwan 2000 Report*. I explained the parallels I saw between the insights the report had given us through scientific study, on the one hand, and the Daoist intuition of the coherence between ecology and economy, on the other. At this point, I expected nods of approval from the young scientists. But in fact, my observation was received with deafening silence. At the end of my talk, I received little more than polite applause. The blank looks and lack of questions told me that somehow I had completely misread the mood of my audience. At first, I couldn't understand why such an obvious link—obvious to me, at least—seemed completely foreign to people who had actually grown up with Daoism. Not until later did I realise that my listeners, with their Western education and experience, didn't want to be associated with the centuries-old traditions of their homeland. To them, Daoism was an outdated view of life that would more likely serve as a brake on progress in Taiwan than as a rock in turbulent times. Where had I heard that before? Was it not Teilhard who, at the beginning of the last century, had had the same experience when he was working in China as a palaeontologist? Neither his Chinese colleagues nor he himself were interested in the Daoist roots of the culture they were living in.

Daoism may have been 2,500 years old, it seemed further away than ever, I realised—even in Taiwan, an island that was close to the birthplace of Daoism yet sufficiently distant to have survived the destruction of the Cultural Revolution. Apparently, the time was not yet ripe for a renewed appreciation of this religious and philosophical legacy.

But it didn't stop me from continuing my search into ways of redressing the balance between ecology and economy. I heard that China planned to steer Hainan, an island in the South China Sea and the smallest province in the People's Republic, into the economic fast lane and turn it into a free-trade zone. With the lessons from Taiwan in mind, I thought it no more than natural to warn against the potential ecological consequences of unbridled economic growth and to point to alternative options. The size and significance of the island seemed to make it an ideal place for a pilot project that might be of some relevance to mainland China as well. Since 1978, the People's Republic had entered a new era under Deng Xiaoping with his Open Door Policy: a capitalist economy led by a communist party. Given the prevailing mantra of welfare growth for the masses, I expected an economic growth spurt. It seemed to me that China shouldn't have to suffer the same ecological pain as Taiwan. So I contacted the Chinese Embassy in the United Kingdom and was invited for a 'long talk' with a member of the embassy staff. Armed with the *Taiwan 2000 Report*, I proceeded to a top Chinese restaurant my host had selected for the occasion. He listened to my story, nodded politely, visibly enjoying an excellent lunch, and let me know that he would discuss my account with his superiors and then get back to me. I never heard from the embassy again. Clearly, ecology was not an issue; it was economy that ruled the political agenda. And since the turn of the century, we have been seeing more and more clearly the terrible effects. Sprawling Chinese cities are covered in a thick layer of smog for ever-longer periods. Rivers are turning black, red and yellow as waste is dumped, legally or otherwise, and algae are growing out of control. I can still picture similar scenes in 1980s Taiwan except that in China the problem is on a much larger scale. And as I witness this now, I continue to regret that my proposals for Hainan didn't make it beyond that embassy official. I can only conclude such ideas were premature.

If there was anything to be learnt from my experience in the corporate world, from the *Taiwan 2000 Report* and from my meeting with the Chinese Embassy, it was that ecology in the political and economic domain was still the black sheep of the family. In the West, 'the environment' was a thorny chapter whose urgency the political and business communities apparently failed to see; while in the Far East, the subject was seen as a direct threat to political stability and the economy. These views seemed hopelessly outdated and a serious threat to the liveability of our planet in the medium term. But I found time and time again that people were not ready for a turnaround.

Still, the *Taiwan 2000 Report* showed that it was possible to put a subject like ecology onto the political and social map. Through persistent pressure, smart networking, the right expertise and valid arguments, it seemed possible to open eyes and sow the seeds of a new, ecological awareness. It inspired me to carry on, to continue drawing attention to the ecological problems that were approaching and, most of all, to look for practical solutions. In the spirit of my educational background at Delft and the proven method of marginal action, I set up the Ecological Management Foundation (EMF) in 1990, so I could focus in a structured manner on restoring the balance between ecology and economy in the policies of government and business. And somewhere in its early life, something special happened: Engelen produced his 1988 documentaries, *The Price of a Miracle*. The episode about Taiwan was aptly called *The Blood of the Earth*, a reference to the important role and symbolic meaning of water in the Daoist view of life. This view is captured very poetically in a passage from the Guan Zi, a compilation of Chinese philosophical texts from around 700 BCE.

Now water is the blood and the breath of the earth, flowing and communicating as if in muscles and veins. Therefore we say water is the preparatory raw material of all things. How do we know that this is so? The answer is that water is yielding, weak, and clean, and likes to wash away the evils of man. This may be called its benevolence. It sometimes looks black, sometimes white; this may be called its essence. When you measure it, you cannot force it to level off at the top, for when the vessel is full it does that by itself. This may be called its rectitude. There is no space into which it will not flow, and when it is level it stops. This may be called its fairness. People all like to go up higher, but water runs to the lowest possible place. This principle of going down to the bottom is the Palace of the Dao, and the instrument of true rulers. The bottom is where water goes and lives.

The role of water fascinated me and over the years it had somehow grown on me. At university, I had become acquainted with water primarily as an abstract reflection of reality, as H2O, so I could understand and create chemical reactions. Besides this, it was simply the substance that came out of the tap and was taken for granted. But inspired by the passage from the Guan Zi, I thought about the phenomenon of water more consciously and realised it is so much more than a molecule or a commodity. It struck me that the water molecules populating our earth and even our bodies to this very day are the exact same molecules that emerged in the universe 12 billion years ago. I still think it's a fascinating notion: water as a silent witness of our past life, as a component of the present and as a blueprint for the future. Water is rightfully considered the blood of the earth. No wonder water plays such a prominent role in so many cultural and religious traditions.

So how come we viewed water as a matter of course? At least, this was the case in the West—elsewhere in the world, the lack of clean water cost many thousands of lives every day. The more I looked at the issues surrounding water in subsequent years, the more I saw the enormous tragedy resulting from unequal access to this substance. With a growing population in the most arid places on earth, I foresaw a global scenario of collapse if we didn't tackle regional water scarcity. Again, the lessons of my past surfaced: quick intervention was paramount and any major breakthrough was unlikely to come exclusively from large, international organisations. It was all I needed to continue on from *The Transformation Factor* and commit my time and energy to the water sector. From the second half of the 1990s, EMF would work on building global awareness of water issues and look for solutions to regional water scarcity. What's more, water in Daoism is associated with the female Yin: it is soft, nurturing, fluid and yet capable of breaking or eroding the toughest material. It occurred to me that my dedication to water would be a splendid way of following up on Guan Yin's message.

What had started as a radical change in my working life had meta-morphosed into an exploratory journey past the Dao and Teilhard and then progressed into a practical mission to reintegrate ecology and economy and improve universal access to water. I had not planned these events—they had simply come about. Was this a masterly example of serendipity? Or was it more?

What is, is, what is not, is not.

The Dao is made because we walk it,

Things become what they are called.

Chapter 2 of the Zhuang Zi

3

The Way to Taibai Shan

Building the First Daoist Ecology Temple

The first time I met Martin Palmer of the Alliance of Religions and Conservation (ARC) was on a summer evening in 2002. A friend had invited me to dinner on behalf of the Dutch Rabobank. The guests were various Dutch and international parties working on the bank's sustainability projects. I was not exactly a project partner but had previously served on a committee set up to advise the board of directors on a sustainable footprint for the bank's financing system. It was one of my attempts to put into practice Thomas Berry's marginal action, an attempt to restore the balance between ecology and economy and to give teeth to my findings in *The Transformation Factor*. On the committee, I pointed out that a cooperative bank that had grown big as a financier of the agricultural sector couldn't get round the issue of water. Agriculture, after all, is a large user of this 'blood of the earth'. Any initiative that could help reduce water consumption in this sector was more than just a drop in the ocean. In response, Rabobank appointed Jean Pierre Sweerts, a biologist by training but increasingly specialised in hydrology.

I had developed a friendship with Jean Pierre and he knew of my interest in the philosophy of life and Daoism in particular. He said there would be some other guests who shared that interest. So there I sat, in the Karel V restaurant in Utrecht, with two British gentlemen to my left and right who introduced themselves as Martin Palmer and Brian Pilkington, Secretary General and Chairman of the Board of

Trustees of the Alliance of Religions and Conservation, respectively. Martin and Brian told me that ARC is a secular organisation in the UK that works together with the major religions worldwide and, based on their respective traditions, develops programmes to promote ecological conservation and environmental awareness. An interesting idea: the connection between religion and nature conservation was unusual to say the least. Yes, we hear that a lot, was the response from Martin and Brian. Secular organisations concerned with nature and the environment didn't exactly think of religious leaders when it came to picking partners. It was better to negotiate agreements with domestic or foreign governments and with multilateral organisations; at least that was the prevailing opinion. But Brian and Martin said that would be an opportunity missed because religious networks cover about 85 per cent of the world population and have a huge influence on social, political, educational and cultural structures, locally as well as nationally. And they are far more stable than many governments. How many monarchies, dictatorships, republics and democracies end up as a footnote in history books, while the religions have weathered the storms of politics for many thousands of years? Add to this the statistic that religious groups manage around 8 per cent of the earth's habitable land, and we arrive at a substantial and sustainable sphere of influence for a global ecological awakening. This realisation was starting to dawn on secular environmental and conservation organisations even if ARC still had a tough job getting all of the parties around the table.

Somewhere between the main course and dessert, my conversation with Martin shifted to Daoism, one of ARC's eleven affiliated religions. Not only could Martin talk with great enthusiasm about ARC's Daoism project, he also turned out to be an authority on this timeless Chinese philosophy and a great admirer. He had lived in China for a while, spoke the language and had written quite a few books about Daoism (among other things), including English translations of the Dao De Jing and Zhuang Zi. But that wasn't our only common interest. Like myself, Martin also had a strong fascination and love for Guan Yin—or in Martin's own inimitable witty way: we fancy the same 1,000-year-old woman. He'd even written a book about the goddess called *The Guan Yin Chronicles: The Myths and Prophecies of the Chinese Goddess of Compassion*. So there she was, Guan Yin. She would not disappear from the dinner table that evening and it was the start of a conversation between Martin and myself that has continued ever since. The evening flew by and marked the beginning of a fruitful collaboration, a valuable friendship and a special, inspiring journey.

In the following years, Martin invited me to several ARC meetings and so I gradually got to know and appreciate the organisation. It was nice to see how a relatively small group of passionate individuals managed to create a growing network of religious, environmental and conservation organisations, based on the idea of motivating people through their religion to deal with the earth in an ecologically responsible way. The essence of this message actually comes very close to the core message of the world's faiths. Respect and care for the earth are, after all, a thread that runs through many scriptures. ARC encourages the religions to become aware of the link and put the lessons learnt into practice by helping them formulate their sustainability ambitions, by fleshing out practical details, by sharing knowledge and, last but not least, by bringing these developments to the attention of secular conservation and aid organisations and facilitating collaboration.

It's perhaps logical and simple enough but easier said than done. I recall many meetings were downright strategy sessions to determine which religious leaders should be approached and how; which alliances could be forged with which secular groups and how; and which authorities should be involved. And ultimately, it's a question of knowing the local flavour and manoeuvring between what are often very divergent interests. I have truly come to admire the way in which Martin and his team have been able to inspire and facilitate a growing network with their own enthusiasm, flexibility and respect for local traditions and needs. I felt ARC's way of working was a good example of marginal action: no pulling, no pushing, no pressuring from within or without, but working together at the margin and inconspicuously creating and tapping into opportunities to engineer change. ARC's Daoism project in China would see into action this way of working and the various strategic considerations in their full complexity. In China, it's difficult to underestimate the role of government: without agreement from the authorities, it's virtually impossible to get anything done there. And even with government approval—or perhaps because of it—it would prove to be a tough job to navigate the complex Chinese social structures.

In due course, I also met the founding father of ARC, HRH Prince Philip. The history of how ARC was born is a great story that reflects the strong will, humour and astuteness of this colourful man. As President of WWF International, Prince Philip had first reached out to faith communities in 1986, in the lead-up to a meeting celebrating the 25th anniversary of WWF International. It was reported that the prince was tired of sitting down with the same people every year. The conservation of nature was in need of a new impulse. How about bringing in religious groups? Martin, at that time Religious Advisor at WWF UK, was just the man to help him with that. He invited five leaders of the world's main religions (Buddhism, Christianity, Hinduism, Islam and Judaism) to the meeting. It was not an easy ride because most of the WWF branches around the world voted against the proposal and WWF US even boycotted the meeting in protest. To them, it was unacceptable that a secular, independent organisation like WWF would associate with religious societies. The only branch to vote in favour was WWF UK. Thanks to Martin, this office was not unfamiliar with the phenomenon of religion. Despite the resistance, there were five extra chairs at the meeting for the religious leaders. And that wasn't all: with the appropriate sense of provocation and staging, Prince Philip and Martin came up with the idea to hold the meeting in Assisi, the very place where Francis of Assisi lived and died. Francis is a Roman Catholic saint from the 12th century who is known chiefly for his love and respect for nature and animals.

All in all, it looked like a guaranteed recipe for an unruly international WWF meeting—fodder for the press, who were present in large numbers. But what had seemed a risky venture turned out to be an unqualified success: for the first time ever, representatives of religious traditions and the top of the environmental and conservation protection community talked about the possibility of collaboration. The outcome was that the five religions formulated key statements about their own role in nature conservation, in line with their own traditions. Moreover, the unprecedented press attention ensured that these new voices were heard in all corners of the world and at every level. In subsequent years, Martin's role as Religious Advisor at WWF UK meant he would not be sitting still as the network grew to nine religions, including the Daoists. Eventually, WWF couldn't cope with the project any longer and it was a logical, next step to set up a separate organisation. This was the birth of ARC in 1995.

Here too, everything was done according to Prince Philip's proven recipe: with a great flourish. ARC had asked religious leaders beforehand what they and their traditions regarded as the main obstacles in a modern, global society. Almost unanimously they cited the mass media, which was dominated by the West and the power of economic forces such as the World Bank. So Prince Philip and Martin made sure that the BBC World Service and World Bank were present when ARC was launched at Windsor Castle. The event made the front page of *The Times*, the BBC would work together with ARC many more times and, in 1997, the World Bank and nine religions formalised their ties in various ARC/World Bank projects.

At key moments, ARC celebrated its achievements and projects in grand style and invariably attracted considerable local and international interest. Prince Philip's presence or just his written support guaranteed there would be ample attention from the press. A growing number of religious as well as secular environmental, conservation and aid organisations became acquainted with ARC's vision and mission and joined up, which is what mattered in the end. The World Bank did so in 1997 with an agreement to collaborate with religions on a project basis. In 2000, the tally of affiliated religions stood at eleven and, in 2008, the United Nations Development Programme (UNDP) announced a partnership with ARC to assist religious organisations in formulating multi-year plans to make their religious traditions more sustainable.

But all the attention and spectacular growth of ARC had another effect. They ensured that the religions were put on the world map as partners in sustainability and social change—not insignificant in a country like China, which was officially communist and non-religious. The authorities had carefully pushed religion to the brink in the previous century and Daoism, having long been dismissed as a backward superstition, in particular. When *The Times* then splashes a photograph across the front page of a Daoist master celebrating the establishment of ARC in 1995, Beijing sits up and takes notice. In Martin's opinion, such incidents are a signal to the Chinese government that Daoism is a legitimate player on the international stage: Daoism is a meaningful force that touches the core of Chinese society.

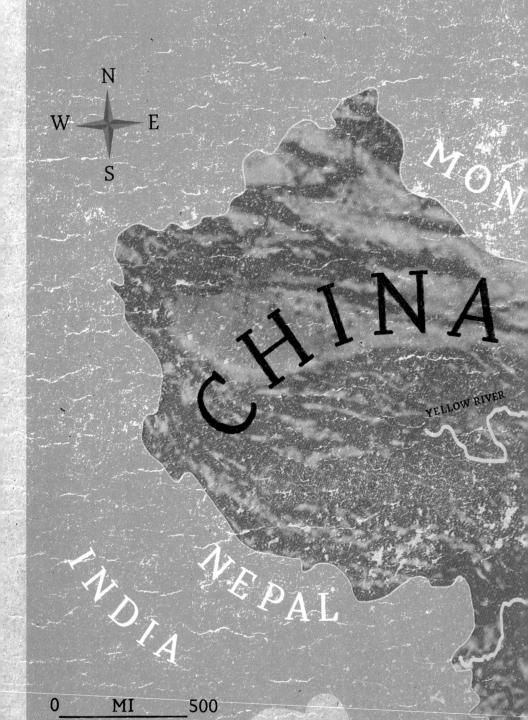

GOLIA

BEIJING

HÉNG SHÀN

XI'AN

TÀI SHÀN

TAIBAI SHÀN

HUÀ SHÀN   SONG SHÀN

QINLING MOUNTAIN RANGE

SHANGHAI

YANGTZE RIVER

HÉNG SHÀN

HONG KONG

SACRED
MOUNTAINS

Sacred Mountains of China

Martin Palmer

The classic Chinese landscape is perhaps one of the best known art forms around the world. Such a scene will almost invariably feature a mountain somewhere in it, often forming the forefront of the picture. Mountains are a key element not just in the artwork of China but in the psyche of the Chinese. From the earliest times, emperors have gone to sacred mountains in order to report to heaven on how they are doing. From earliest times, hermits and recluses have sought peace and spirituality on the mountains. From ancient times, the mountains have been the place where herbs were gathered for the creation of proper traditional Chinese medicine. And on the mountains immortals, deities and human beings have lived side by side with nature—flora and fauna.

Traditionally, there are nine major sacred mountains: five Daoist and four Buddhist. The five Daoist mountains mark out the traditional compass of the Chinese, namely north (Heng Shan), south (another Heng Shan), west (Hua Shan), east (Tai Shan) and centre (Song Shan). Each has its place in the mythology and teachings of Daoism.

The traditional maps of China differ in one very significant way from maps anywhere else in the world. On ancient Chinese maps, the south is always placed at the top, with north relegated to the bottom. This was no accident or quirk born of perverseness. The reason is simple: south is the direction of the Divine and the powerful. Only the emperor was allowed to face south, all those around him had to face north.

In the West, we see the East as the direction of the spiritual—of Eden or the Holy land, of India or the 'mysteries of the East' such as Egypt. In China, west is the direction of the spiritual—the great legendary teacher Lao Zi 'went west' when he despaired of China, dictating his great classic, the Dao De Jing, at the Gate to the West—now known as Louguan Tai and the home of Master Ren. When the Emperor Ming (58–75 CE) dreamt of a Golden Man in the West, he knew that this meant a new religion or spiritual tradition and duly, so the legend says, sent envoys to find this teacher. Back came Buddhism—from the West.

Beyond these nine major mountains, there are many others of great antiquity and significance. Chief amongst these would be Qing Cheng

Shan in Sichuan Province, where Master Zhang Dao Ling encountered Lao Zi and was given the power to start the organised movement of Daoism as a religion, and Taibai Shan, where the Daoist ecological temple has been built. Mao Shan, site of the Daoist conference which developed the Eight-Year Plan, is another very important sacred mountain.

Below these come the local sacred mountains and there are hundreds of these.

Nature Protection

The significance of the sacred mountains became only too clear during the worst ravages of the Cultural Revolution between 1966 and 1976. Their sacred nature often led local people to protect them from the worst attacks and this is why they are, still to this day, more ecologically significant than other mountains which did not have this protection.

In the late 1990s, ARC conducted a survey of the nine major mountains and showed that, where religious activities were still permitted and monks or nuns were in residence, the environment was as a result better protected.

The sacred mountains differ in their style and this tells us a great deal about the difference between Daoism—that is to say indigenous religious tradition—and a foreign religion such as Buddhism. To climb a Buddhist sacred mountain is to travel as a visitor. The monasteries along the way tend to be large and dominant in the landscape. They provide places from which to admire the view and to enjoy the natural beauty. Daoist mountains are different. The monasteries and temples are much smaller and often seem to emerge from the very rocks themselves, moulding themselves to the shapes and scale of the landscape. They are not places from which to look out and admire the views because you are not the observer. Instead you are part of the mountain and, by walking the Path—the Way (Dao) of the mountain, you become part of the Way.

Climbing the Mountain

Daoist mountains are places for reflection and meditation at every stage. Hua Shan in Shaanxi Province is a perfect example of this. To climb this—or any—mountain is to rise to communication with the gods, for, in classical Chinese belief, the mountain is a cosmic pillar, facilitating interaction between the material world and the spiritual.

This walking the Path is fundamental to visiting a sacred mountain. Indeed, I have heard from Daoist monks that their main objection to the growth of cable cars on sacred mountains is that it not only disrupts the spiritual flow of the mountain—*feng shui*—but stops people walking. As one monk said on Tai Shan: you walk to know humility. If you fly to the top by cables, you think you are an immortal or a god. Well, you are not!

On Hua Shan, the Path winds past the shrines to the local earth gods and the protect… 'ities of the mountain. Legends and stories fill every turning in the Path; every large rock has its myth. These legends reflect the core beliefs of the mass of ordinary people, the peasants of China, for whom life has always been tough. In these legends, the powerful are outwitted and the poor protected.

Along the path up Hua Shan, you will find Chinese characters carved into the living rock. Often, it will be a simple character such as Heaven. Other times, it will be a poem, written by a famous poet and inscribed here by admirers. The very characters of Chinese writing are in themselves sacred. They not only express the ideas contained within them, but are themselves part of what they express. Thus, a character for Heaven is heavenly; a character for good fortune is in itself fortunate. In combining writing with landscape, the Chinese bring together two powerful strands of the sacred beauty of the climb: moments of reflection and introspection on a climb from Earth to Heaven.

Dong Tien

As you climb the mountain, you might come across a *dong tien* or grotto. These are Heaven Caves and refer to what are in fact the oldest nature reserves in China. Founded by Daoists starting in the 4th to 6th centuries CE, these are places where heaven and earth touch. Sacred places are sacred because of the abundance and magnificence of nature present there and the sense of spirituality. These

dong tien have also been amongst the earliest examples of community ecology. Established by Daoism, they have been maintained and protected by the local communities down the centuries and their survival to this day is due to both their sacredness and their democratic management. Across China, over thirty specific places with *dong tien* are listed. But there are probably many others. Taibai Shan is one of them.

While Hua Shan is a Daoist sacred mountain, it is also ecumenical—as are virtually all the sacred mountains. Here you will find not just Daoist deities but Buddhist ones as well—especially Guan Yin. A mixture of Daoist, Buddhist and perhaps even older deities are to be found, as these mountains have been sacred for thousands of years. They pre-date any of the existing formal religions, but perhaps owe their holiness to the earliest and possibly earthiest of world religions: shamanism.

Climbing further, we come to yet another reminder of the antiquity of sacred China. High on the side of a cliff on East Peak, there appears to be a gigantic handprint. This is reputed to be the handprint of a giant sent to help the heroic demi-god Yu the Great. In one of the most popular of Chinese ancient myths, the world was threatened by massive floods. The Yellow River had burst its banks and was inundating China, sweeping away homes and farmland. The Emperor Yao, one of the hero emperors of antiquity and a model for Confucian virtues, summoned Yu the Great to battle with these waters. Yu was almost certainly a shamanistic figure for he could turn into a bear at will. Together with his faithful friend the Dragon, he carved new pathways for the river, built dykes and dams to control the waters and, eventually after ten years of unremitting struggle, channelled the waters of the Yellow River into a safe new course. In the process of doing this, he had to split Hua Shan in half because it was blocking the new pathway to the ocean. On East Peak, you can see the imprint of the hand of the giant sent by Heaven to assist Yu in dividing the great mountain.

Just as Chinese religion has not one belief system but at least three major ones and according to Chinese tradition, five, so the mountain also has more than one peak. This is important to remember about Chinese religion. There is no one answer. The Chinese operate happily with a variety of belief systems, combining elements of shamanism, Confucianism, Daoism, Buddhism and at times Christianity as well. Asking which is the more important is often not appropriate, as is asking which of the five peaks of Hua Shan is the most important. They are all important because they are all different. Together they add up to the total experience.

Lao Zi

On the upper reaches, between the South Peak and the West Peak, is a temple to Lao Zi, the fabled founder figure of Daoism. Probably a historical figure of the 6th to 5th centuries BCE, he later became mythologised into one of the Three Primal Beings of the Cosmos. In one of his forms, he is the maker of the pills of immortality and now he is the God of Ecology for the Daoists.

The Path seems to end at this temple, yet just beyond this high point it wanders on again. It is hard to tell when you have arrived at the end of the Path, the Dao of Hua Shan, for there are always paths leading on elsewhere. In this way, it reflects perfectly the quest for the Dao and the elusiveness of that quest—indeed the elusiveness of the sacred itself. As Lao Zi's reputed book the Dao De Jing puts it:

The Dao that can be talked about
is not the true Dao.
The name that can be named
is not the eternal Name.
Everything in the universe
comes out of Nothing.
Nothing—the nameless
is the beginning;
While Heaven, the mother
is the creatrix of all things.
Follow the nothingness of the Dao,
and you can be like it, not needing
anything seeing the wonder
and the root of everything.
And even if you cannot grasp
this nothingness, you can still see
something of the Dao in everything...

Chapter 1, Dao De Jing,

translated by Kwok, Palmer and Ramsay

It shouldn't surprise us that such a signal sometimes came from the outside world. After a century of systematic repression and destruction of all that smacked of religion, China had simply lost almost every source of information about Daoism. Temples and texts had been destroyed, masters forced to renounce their religious practices—or worse. Knowledge and acknowledgment basically had to come from abroad—from Taiwan for example, where some Chinese masters had escaped to and where Daoism went into 'exile'. Or from Western libraries and centres of expertise, where studies and passages of text had been preserved. This didn't mean that knowledge could be ferried across the border at will. There was always a delicate balance between knowledge sharing and unwelcome interference in government affairs, something Martin experienced the moment he set foot on Chinese soil.

In the early 1990s, Martin had visited Hua Shan, one of the five sacred mountains in Daoist tradition. He was touched by its beauty but also very aware that the religious dimension was almost invisible. So when the contours of ARC as a separate organisation began to emerge in 1993 and the first budgets allowed it, he forged an initial link with the China Daoist Association. He told me about their first meeting, in the middle of winter in an unheated, ramshackle building that had once been the celebrated White Cloud Temple. The Daoists had recently 'recovered' the temple from the authorities. They had lost it during the Cultural Revolution, when the monks had been chased away and the complex had been put to several uses, none remotely associated with Daoism—as was the fate of many sanctuaries. Now that religions in China were given some more room for manoeuvre, the government was gradually returning some sanctuaries to the original owners. But the abbot and his monks were too strapped for cash even to light a simple fire, let alone renovate an entire building. The poverty which the Daoists—and indeed many religious groups—grappled with never penetrated as deeply as on the freezing cold day of that first meeting. Martin sat down on a chair that was about to fall apart and talked with the secretary of the Daoist Association, Master Zhang Yiju. They got on really well and Martin had no trouble pointing out to him the ecological aspects that are so closely tied in with Daoist philosophy. Master Zhang picked up on it and a few months later the Daoists had worked out their faith statement on ecology, a prerequisite for joining ARC in 1995.

By 1996, ARC had acquired the freedom to initiate a study in China on the five sacred mountains and their relationship with nature conservation and biodiversity. Researchers Tjalling Halbertsma and Peter Zhao literally covered the sacred mountains in every direction so they could map the flora and fauna, culture, landscape and religion of these regions. It was a two-year project with plenty of hitches because this is where the Chinese government threw its weight about: the researchers were arrested several times on suspicion of illegal, subversive activities. Martin thought it was because the government had no idea what exactly they were doing and saw them as a threat. In the eyes of government officials, ecology and religion could at best be regarded as folkloric hobbies that stood in the way of progress. In a country singularly focused on growing the economy and preserving social harmony, environmental pollution was not on the agenda. Moreover, if religion should take the lead in identifying societal problems such as the loss of nature—and so fail to respect the government mandate and perhaps disrupt social harmony—the world would be topsy-turvy. This was reason enough to rein in the two researchers. It took Martin quite some effort to keep them on the rails but the final outcome was well worth it. In 1998, ARC was able to report that land managed by Daoists had a healthier biodiversity than other land. With this information, ARC persuaded the Chinese authorities to return 124 sites to Daoist communities on Hua Shan and to give them a say in managing the sites. On top of that, the Daoists could keep 10 per cent of the proceeds from tickets sales to give them their own source of income. This deal was a significant milestone in that it recognised the role of Daoism in nature conservation and gave Daoist temple communities the means to escape poverty and renovate sacred places.

These achievements were as promising as the next project was troublesome, when ARC was at great pains to arrange the necessary funds. This was a follow-up project aimed at endangered animals and traditional Chinese medicines. In 2000 and in partnership with ARC, the Daoists issued an important statement against the use of products derived from endangered species for use in traditional Chinese medicines. In their philosophy, medicine designed to make the body healthy (i.e. to restore the balance in the body between yin and yang) can never come from products yielded by species on the verge of extinction. Such medicine won't work or will backfire. But conservation organisations, despite their passion for the protection of endangered animals, didn't believe in this approach or didn't want to sit down with a religious group. The millennium celebrations in Kathmandu, Nepal, in the year 2000 could have offered a way out. ARC was organising this event together with WWF International to celebrate the contribution made by religion to the conservation of nature. The Daoists would be coming too. But now the Chinese government stirred. A few weeks before the event, the Pope announced a number of canonisations, including 124 saints in China, practically all from abroad. The Chinese government saw this as a provocation and as interference in domestic affairs. Their response was to forbid the Daoists from travelling to Nepal. Martin later told me that, for a brief moment, his hopes that ARC would ever be able to help the Daoists on the road to sustainability and to the core of Chinese society were beginning to fade.

And then there was that evening in 2002 when Guan Yin brought us together. It would be two more years before Martin told me about the Taibai Shan project. Around that time, WWF Netherlands knocked on ARC's door. In a joint project with WWF China, they were building an eco-resort on Taibai Shan (Great White Mountain), a mountain in the centrally located Qinling mountain range, which separates northern from southern China. Qinling is home to the endangered giant panda, the black-and-white bear that adorns the WWF logo, making it *the* symbol for the worldwide protection of nature. WWF Netherlands financed projects to protect the panda and the eco-resort was intended to generate sustainable tourism and a steady source of income for the panda's habitat. Just by chance, the Dutch had stumbled upon what seemed to be the remains of an old temple complex. ARC's Tjalling Halbertsma and Peter Zhao were invited to assess the situation. To their amazement, they found a very powerful sacred site.

Since time immemorial, there had been a temple at the foot of a pilgrim trail up Mount Taibai. Like many other temples and sanctuaries, it didn't survive the destruction inflicted during the Cultural Revolution. But the place was still regarded as sacred. Apparently, Mao's followers at the time didn't dare destroy the sacred Iron Armour Tree (Tiejiashu), which stood by the temple complex as a shepherd of Daoist tradition and guardian of pilgrims. 'Whoever touches the tree will be doomed' would have gone through the minds of the Red Guards, the fanatic paramilitary social movement of youths who didn't usually shun violence. At the end of the last century, when religion in China acquired some breathing room, the local community put up a structure to serve as a makeshift temple. Further research showed that the temple site fell under the jurisdiction of the Louguan Tai temple, where according to legend Lao Zi wrote the Dao De Jing. Martin had already been in touch with the abbot of Louguan Tai for another project and links were easily renewed.

ARC, WWF and Master Ren, the vice-abbot of Louguan Tai who recognised the potential, drew up a plan to turn the temple complex on Taibai Shan into a Daoist Ecology Temple and combine it with the construction of an Ecology Education Centre. Under this plan, Daoist masters from all corners of China would be able to use the Ecology Temple and Education Centre to learn how to apply ecological principles to the management of their own temples. They could then be an example to their own, local communities. Together with the WWF eco-resort, Taibai Shan was to become the epicentre of a drive to make Daoist temples throughout China more sustainable, thus stimulating ecological awareness in China and facilitating sustainable tourism. I didn't need much time to consider Martin's request if I would be willing to support this project financially: what better way to put into practice my passion for ecology and Daoism?

So from 2004 onwards, work on the design and realisation of the temple proceeded with feverish haste. In a command economy like China, it's crucial to involve the authorities in any kind of plans, building or otherwise. Even in remote regions like Taibai Shan, government has a big finger in the pie. In this case, the location of the mountain in a remote, relatively poor region played right into the hands of the project initiators because, from an economic growth angle, the provincial government was very willing to grant planning permission and back the project. ARC and WWF could count on the China Daoist Association and Shaanxi Province as partners and the work would be done by local contractors.

The lynchpin of the project was Dr He Xiaoxin, ARC's Director of Chinese Programmes and researcher at the University of Manchester with a PhD in traditional Chinese architecture from Wuhan University.

I first met her at the ARC offices, still in Manchester at that time. Of modest build and appearance, with lively and enquiring eyes betraying passion and perseverance, she is a fountain of energy and knowledge. Her background in that particular architecture and her Chinese roots made her a vital link between ARC and Taibai Shan and allowed her to give a strong impetus to the design of the Ecology Temple. In that design, she meticulously followed the contours and symmetry of the temple that had stood there before it was laid to waste. Sadly, along the way, it transpired that the path back to the old temple had been cut off permanently by China's recent history, as part of the old temple site had been granted to the State Forestry Administration of the People's Republic of China during Mao's reign. That section was off limits so one of the two buildings that were supposed to flank the temple could not be built in the desired spot. Many years later, Xiaoxin told me how disappointed she was that the loss of land had upset the essential symmetry in the original design. The same was true of the makeshift structure that in the original design was supposed to have been replaced by a new building. At the last minute, the local policymakers decided to keep the old temple. Once again, it was easier said than done.

A key element of every Daoist temple is an incense burner where people offer sacrifices to the gods, ask routine as well as deeper questions about life, and pray for help and prosperity. In my own case, the incense burner of the first Daoist Ecology Temple is closely intertwined with a personal story. The autumn of 2004 was dominated by another event that has marked the rest of my life. In October, I lost my eldest daughter, Anneke, to cancer. This is when I discovered that the deepest sense of grief and despair can go hand in hand with the most enlightening insights. One of the most valuable memorials to my daughter came to me via ARC. Martin explained that in China the incense burner in a temple is donated by an outsider. He suggested I should be the donor and I should dedicate the burner to my daughter. I continue to be grateful for his suggestion and I find solace in the poignant reminder that this incense burner has been a source of inspiration and contemplation for so many others to this very day. For the design of the burner, I worked closely together with Xiaoxin. She asked me to characterise my daughter in a few words and, with the help of a local Chinese artist, used that as the basis for the design. I saw the designs develop, of course, but for the final result I had to wait until the opening of the temple, expected in 2005.

In the autumn of that year, the time had come: the temple was nearing completion and everything was ready for the inauguration ceremony. Martin, his wife Victoria Finlay, as well as several relatives and friends joined me on the flight to Beijing and then Xian, where we boarded a bus several days later taking us to faraway Taibai Shan. Martin proved to be a fabulous tour guide, showing us temples and museums along the way. Most of us had never been to China but Martin's amazing knowledge and humorous narrative made a faraway country seem pretty close. On our arrival at Xian Airport, we were welcomed by Peter Zhao, ARC's China expert and researcher since the early days. He now coordinated the project locally. He warned us that we shouldn't expect a finished temple—in fact, the roof still had to be completed. We got on the bus to Taibai Shan and sat down only to discover that the doors were also missing. The walls still had to go up and they still had to put in a floor. By the time we arrived, it was clear nothing had been built. Not a single stone had been laid! Let's just say there were big sighs all round from my fellow passengers. We decided not to get worked up; we assumed there would be a good explanation and that works had been delayed rather than shelved. The next day would after all be a festive occasion with an inauguration ceremony on the programme, perhaps not for the temple itself, but for that piece of earth where it should have been built.

Although I was disappointed at having come such a long way to inaugurate a temple that wasn't there—at least not yet—I found my first encounter with the temple site impressive all the same. This is where we would make a material contribution to the restoration of a time-honoured tradition that, in my eyes, could be so beneficial—not only for China but for the rest of the world too. This is where ARC's mission to unite religion and ecological conservation would become tangible. And this is where my endeavour to link ecology and economy would be cemented in stone, in unexpected fashion perhaps but right in line with my personal interests and outlook on life. There wasn't much for us to see as yet unless the lush, unspoilt wilderness around the temple site was a reference to the Daoist link with nature.

Awakening to a Daoist Ecological Dream

Master Ren Xingzhi

Master Ren comes from a family of once very wealthy bankers but the family fortunes suffered through various upheavals—the fall of the last dynasty, known as the Qing, in 1911; the warlord period that followed; the Japanese invasion from 1936 to 1945; the civil war and of course the rise of communism.

In the early 1980s, when Master Ren was around nineteen years old, he read a famous novel called *She Diao Ying Xiong Zhuan* (Legend of the Eagle Shooting Hero). A key figure in the novel is a famous fighter—the Daoist monk Master Chongyang. This character awoke an interest in him in what Daoism was all about. At that stage, he had no interest in or knowledge of Daoism and the last thing he or indeed his family ever expected was that he would want to become a Daoist monk!

Triggered by his interest in the hero from the book, he started to explore what Daoism taught. Ten years later, in 1991, he became a monk—Daoism answered something within him.

His interest in ecology came from his practice as a monk of rising early in the morning to meditate in the open air. He noticed that, as the sun rose, steam rose from the trees. This sense of nature in balance—of yin and yang—was reinforced by his reading Master Zi Yang's classic book on the Dao, with its focus on balance and harmony. From this came his idea of helping people reconnect with nature—hence the notion of 'forest bath', which started his work with WWF.

Master Ren Xingzhi is the Supervising Master of the Louguan Tai Daoist Temple and Vice President of the Shaanxi Daoist Association. He tells us about a dream come true.

As the master at the Louguan Tai Temple in Xian, I have had the privilege to supervise the development of the Tian Xie Yuan forest bathhouse and the Tiejia Daoist Ecology Temple on Taibai Shan. It has been—and still is—a very inspiring experience that woke me up to the beauty and power of the ecological dimension of Daoism. It is a journey I would like to share here.

Once upon a time, there was a Daoist temple on Taibai Mountain, south-west of the ancient capital of Xian. It was originally called the Tiejiashu Taibai Temple and was built in the early years of our Common Era. The temple hosted the three gods of Taibai Shan and worshipped the Tiejia god as a Ling Guan (the guardian deity of Daoism).

Every year, between 9 June and 9 July in the Chinese lunar calendar, all temples on the mountain would jointly host a big temple fair. At this fair, merchant and religious activities went hand in hand and many people would carry out their pilgrimage to the top of the mountain. The scene was said to be spectacular.

The Tiejiashu Temple was located on the route the pilgrims took to get to the top of the mountain. It was a resting stop for them and also the first temple on their way to the mountain top. Historically, the temple enjoyed great popularity and conducted numerous religious activities. Many religious followers and mountain climbers would pay a visit. The temple was also one of the oldest temples honouring the Taibai gods in China.

The temple had the Taibai mountain as a backdrop and a river flowing alongside—*feng shui* at its best. The trees around it were ancient and tall. The Tiejia (or Iron Armour) tree in front of the temple wore the lushest crown and its branches were decorated by passing believers with red ribbons and ropes as tokens of prayer for happiness and blessings. The Tiejia tree belongs to the *Fagaceae* family and is about three thousand years old. It grows very slowly and, as the name suggests, its bark is as hard as iron armour. The residents of Taibai Mountain considered the tree as a marshal guarding the Taibai gods, and the tree itself was worshipped along with the gods.

According to older residents who lived nearby, there was a Daoist monk, whose family name ironically was Mao, residing in the temple before the 1960s. When the Cultural Revolution broke out, he was forced to leave and the temple was subsequently abandoned and fell into disrepair. In the late 1980s, residents and believers voluntarily donated money and worked to refurbish the temple. They built a few simple rooms to host their gods.

In the early 1990s, local residents requested the reopening of the temple. In order to regulate all religious activities, the local Administration of Religious Affairs agreed to put the Louguan Tai Temple in charge of the temple and sent a resident Daoist to run its daily activities. In the autumn of 2002, seven rooms were built in the temple, three rooms in the middle to host the Taibai gods and the remainder to accommodate the residing Daoist monk.

In 2002, I happened to meet Dr Liu Xiaohai, the deputy director of WWF China at that time. From my conversation with Dr Liu, I learnt that WWF was building a holiday eco-lodge together with Houzhenzi Forest Station. The income from the lodge would be used for panda conservation as part of the WWF 'Gift to the Earth 2003' project. Dr Liu told me about the environmental movement overseas and I was greatly intrigued. I told him about my plans to build a 'forest bathhouse' around the temple. A forest bathhouse can best be described as an open site in the forest where people can come for a rest, a moment of contemplation away from the poisonous hectic of daily life, especially in the city—a cleansing experience of peace and connection with nature. The forest bathhouse had always been one of my dreams. For many years, I had been trying to find a suitable location and make that dream come true. Ultimately, I chose the site where the Tiejiashu Temple stood. In the autumn of 2003, Dr Liu brought the director of WWF to Louguan and asked me to provide them with a working proposal for my forest bathhouse idea. WWF was going to use the forest bathhouse as its 'Gift to the Earth 2004'.

I then researched some relevant Daoist classics and put forward several basic ideas. First, the Daoist teachings on health preservation advocate simplicity and peaceful integration with the surrounding environment. Second, the bathhouse had to reflect the Daoist emphasis on non-doing and harmony between humanity and heaven. Third, the bathhouse needed to forge a close contact with nature and reflect Lao Zi's teaching of 'embracing moderation and reducing desires'. The forest bathhouse was to incorporate these teachings.

With just some rough ideas, I went to see Professor Fan Guangchun to ask him for his assistance. After many discussions, Prof. Fan suggested that we should conduct a field trip with a few Daoist experts. In May 2004, we invited five specialists from Shaanxi Academy of Social Sciences, Shaanxi Teaching University and Xian Daily to visit the Tiejiashu Temple and assess its surrounding environment. They helped to draft a name for my forest bathhouse, calling it Tian Xie Yuan, which means Garden of Heavenly Harmony. It reflects the Daoist idea of harmony between nature, heaven and humanity and advocates a healthy state for the body and the spirit. The bathhouse thus aims to achieve ultimate harmony between the body, mind and Dao.

As construction of the forest bathhouse started in November 2004, the Tiejiashu Temple resumed its official status so that religious activities could take place. It was put under the management of the Louguan Tai Temple and I was to be in charge of its operation. Tian Xie Yuan forest bathhouse was completed in the spring of 2005. It was a dream come true for me. Since then, I have established a great friendship with Taibai Mountain.

At the same time, through the director of Taibai Houzhenzi Forest

Station, Mr Xing Xiaoyu, I met Mr Zhao Xiaomin, the then representative and deputy in China of the Alliance of Religions and Conservation (ARC). Subsequently, I had the opportunity to meet Mr Martin Palmer, the secretary general of ARC, Mr Allerd Stikker, the director of the Dutch Ecological Management Foundation (EMF), and Dr He Xiaoxin, the senior project manager of ARC's China programme at the time. They were involved in the reconstruction of the original Tiejiashu Temple in accordance with its original design. Together, we developed the plan, design and rebuilding of the temple and formally changed its name to Taibai Shan Tiejia Daoist Ecology Temple in order to reflect the temple's conservation ideals. With the assistance of ARC, a generous donation from Mr Stikker and the Louguan Tai Temple as the main supervisor and planner, Houzhenzi Forest Station embarked on rebuilding parts of the temple.

In the autumn of 2005, construction began on Taibai Hall and the major shrine. The rebuild took longer than expected and in 2006 the temple was far from ready. Nevertheless, in July of that year, the Daoist Research Centre of the Shaanxi Academy of Social Sciences and the Louguan Tai Temple, with ARC and EMF as sponsors, hosted the first Daoist ecology workshop at the temple site, thus opening a new chapter for Daoist conservation education.

The temple was finished in 2007.

Mr Stikker placed a special incense burner in the Taibai Hall in honour of his deceased daughter. Since then, the temple has become a spiritual residence for his daughter and a spiritual haven for his family.

At the entrance to the site, the famous, thousand-year-old Armour Tree stood like a loyal, stately landmark, having survived the Cultural Revolution. By tradition, pilgrims on their way up the mountain tie a red ribbon to the tree to seek a blessing for a safe journey, and the tree was covered in ribbons. Some steps alongside the tree then led us to the temple site. It turned out to be just a rough stretch of grass the size of a football field. Somewhere in the distant past, in the middle of the woods on the slopes of Mount Taibai, some trees must have been felled to make way for the original temple. With a bit of imagination, you could still see the contours. The makeshift temple which the local population had built appeared to be part of the U-shape characterising a traditional Daoist temple complex. Immediately opposite stood an old, wooden shed that had seen better days. Inside were garden tools and other objects but, going by the jungle of weeds, it was hardly ever used. Further down, at right angles to the shed and temple, the earth had been dug up in a good-sized rectangle, apparently only recently because grass and weeds had not yet taken root. I understood this was where the temple would be erected. I still found it hard to believe that such a messy piece of earth should have been home to a colourful sanctuary, but I saw it as a hopeful sign of things to come.

When we arrived, we were welcomed by a stocky, jovial Chinese man with a very friendly face and jet black hair tied in a topknot. From his plain, dark blue robe and something like white, knee-length leggings, I could make out he was a Daoist master. It was in fact Master Ren, the Daoist abbot who had embraced and formulated the idea of an Ecology Temple. He was the vice-abbot of the Louguan Tai Temple in Xian and would run the new temple once it was completed. I was struck by the mild-mannered and friendly character of this man and, from the interpretation provided by Peter Zhao, I could tell that Master Ren had a healthy dose of humour. We drank tea in Chinese style and talked about the inauguration ceremony that was on the programme for the next day. After the ceremony, we would meet the contractor and relevant government officials to discuss the building delay.

We were greeted by the sun's rays on a chilly October inauguration day. The temple site had been specially adapted for the occasion. The temple itself was decorated with flags and between the buildings stood a long table covered with a bright yellow tablecloth. There were fruit bowls, candles and instruments on the table as well as some paraphernalia I didn't immediately recognise. Right in front of the table, there was a rug spread out on the patchy grass. To the left and right, monks and nuns moved about in dark blue robes. It was almost impossible to distinguish the men and women, with their pinned-up hair and hats; only when they came close could you tell the difference from the softer features of the nuns. To my surprise, Chinese people and the odd tourist kept coming and going throughout the ceremony. Martin explained that it was customary to have local residents and the occasional outsider join in for part of the ceremony. Depending on the traditions observed by the master who leads the ceremony, the whole ritual can take many hours. During that entire time, the temple stays open to visitors, so it's not unusual that they pass across the stage once in a while.

It was an exceptionally colourful and exotic occasion but the thing that caught my attention was standing on a small table a bit further along: the incense burner, dedicated to my daughter. Cast in reddish copper, robust yet refined, it was sitting there gleaming in the sun. And cast in relief was a text in English as well as Chinese. Around the edge, elegant horses were in full gallop, representing one of my daughter's passions and, according to Daoist tradition, carrying the soul of the deceased back to eternity. Here was Anneke embodied in copper. It was very moving and I realised that my family would be linked to this place forever. I was brought back from my reverie by the sound of singing, drums and bells. Monks and nuns paraded from the temple, dressed in deep red robes and black satin hats, and gathered around the rug by the yellow table. A master in a light blue robe, decorated with yin-yang and other Daoist symbols, led the ceremony. He recited a number of texts, kept rolling a long piece of wood covered with Chinese characters in his hands, and every now and then picked up an object or burnt an incense stick. He was assisted by two monks in peach-coloured robes, who were rhythmically tapping a drum and a singing bowl. At some distance, and occasionally coming to their aid, Master Ren supervised the scene like an accomplished director. Of course, we had no idea what was being said and sung, but Martin was able to give us a general idea. He said that the purpose of this thousand-year-old ritual was to invite the gods to bless and safeguard the place. The dances, songs, and parades are a way of invoking the gods and creating a link between heaven and earth. At one point the priests were dancing through the constellations, stepping gently on stars in space. From the corner of my eye, I noticed a slightly older Chinese man in a cap busying himself with a spade. It was rather comical to see a site worker, drummed up at the last minute, digging a hole as a token of where the temple should have been.

At the end of the ceremony, Martin, Peter and I were invited to a meeting with the building contractor, a representative of the provincial government and Master Ren. With due ceremony and apologies, the truth came out: construction could not begin because the current design of the temple was too small.

"Too small?"

"Yes, three gods will each get a place in the temple as statues and need more space to separate them than the current design allows. The temple should be a few yards wider."

"The gods need more space between them?"

"That's right, because they don't get along. A few extra yards will preserve peace and harmony in the temple."

"You don't say!"

"Yes, and that of course costs money and is why construction hasn't begun."

"And how much does the extra space cost?"

They cited a figure but I had already decided the temple shouldn't founder on the issue of money—it had to be built one way or the other. Before I knew it, I had promised the necessary sum. But I did want to know why they needed three gods.

"Why not just one?"

"Oh no, because these three gods guard the Big White Mountain: the Northern God as a protector deity, the Emperor God in his Imperial yellow robes; and the Eastern God for blessings. Each of them needs a place in the temple. And besides, they work in shifts!"

The party left and Martin burst out laughing.

"Well, Allerd, here's karma for you. In your days as a businessman, you've cracked some tough nuts with uncompromising trade unions and now you're stuck with a bunch of unionised Gods!"

Still, the state of affairs at that moment did raise some questions. That evening, in the WWF eco-lodge where we were staying, Martin and I had a long talk. How was it possible that we in Europe were so poorly informed about what was going on with Taibai Shan? Martin explained that the entire venture had been a complicated process from the outset and that ARC coordinator Peter Zhao had been given an almost impossible task. First of all, the project had a distinctly foreign flavour of course. To be sure, the plan had been developed in collaboration with the local Daoist Association, had received approval from the provincial government and would use local builders, but the all-important financing was in foreign hands. Martin compared it to paying for St Paul's Cathedral with foreign funds, which at the very least would have thrown all those involved, including all of London, into turmoil.

And then there was the tricky act of balancing the interests of government agencies and state-regulated organisations like the Daoist Association, on the one hand, against the interests of the Daoist community, on the other. In China, it is practically impossible to do anything without the approval, or at least knowledge, of the government. Not that local residents, organisations and religious groups are in any hurry to involve the authorities in their wheeling and dealing: there's considerable distrust and the Chinese have many subtle and creative ways of coping, as I have come to learn. Because of the distrust, foreigners are viewed with some suspicion—even, or perhaps especially, when they come with money. They are in the first instance seen as just an extension of government. On top of this, there is a complex relationship between the state-regulated Daoist Associations and local religious communities. The relationship between Daoists who are affiliated with the Association and those who are not isn't exactly amicable. In practice, an affiliation with the Association is all but a prerequisite for a new temple, but among the older generation of masters especially, the distrust of a government interfering in religious affairs is almost palpable. No doubt, the experience of the previous century still weighs heavily on them.

These complex relationships determined the flow of information and meant that ARC and Peter Zhao were operating in a minefield. Add to that the widespread Confucian practice of giving your clients and superiors desirable rather than realistic answers, and you start seeing an outline of the Taibai Shan scenario. Martin and I concluded that this way of doing business would be completely unacceptable in the Netherlands or the United Kingdom, but that it was actually a very educational experience. Not only had we gained insight into the unwritten rules of Chinese culture and communication first-hand, but it made us rethink our own traditions and prejudices. While we in the West like to speak of *priority*, people in China are more focused on time. Everything happens in its own time; it's pointless to fight or hasten destiny—these are the rules. Or as Martin expressed this Daoist principle: don't try to run it, try to flow with it. It's the principle of *wu-wei* and an insight that has grown to be very precious to me over the years.

And it was badly needed in the Taibai Shan project because the opening planned for the following year again fell through. The winter of 2006 was unexpectedly early and severe, making the Taibai Shan region simply too remote for the building contractor. Construction fell behind once more. But the year after, in June 2007, the hour had finally come. We flew back to Taibai Shan, this time with my entire family, for the inauguration of a tangible Daoist Ecology Temple and Education Centre. And what a difference from two years earlier! Where there had just been a pile of dug-up earth, an imposing temple had arisen, a few yards above the ground and accessible via a wide flight of steps—an austere brick structure with dark-red wooden frames and posts. In front of the entrance, right in the middle and half-way up the steps, stood the incense burner, adorned with flowers. The temple interior was a bit of a shock: very plain and unpainted, clearly an unfinished work. At the same time, it didn't really surprise us any longer. And frankly, I found an austere and uncluttered interior quite beautiful and peaceful. The three gods on their thrones also needed a splash of paint. For the occasion, a cloth had been draped over their heads, which made them look rather like ghostly apparitions staring blankly beyond the vague line of the horizon. We came to the conclusion that the lack of any specific form was actually very Daoistic and restful. Without any colour or expression, they didn't yet have that sometimes ferocious and forbidding appearance so characteristic of idols in Daoist temples. It was hard to imagine that the threesome didn't get on.

We were again welcomed by Master Ren, the proud abbot of the brand-new temple. It was a pleasant reunion and when he greeted me, he gave a long and firm handshake—for just a moment, I felt Guan Yin's presence. Martin later told me that such an intense handshake was a special sign of friendship and bonding with Daoist tradition.

That evening, Master Ren invited us to a barbecue on the square in front of the eco-lodge where we were staying again. The nuns and monks who would take care of the inauguration ceremony the next day were also present. I was very curious to know how this evening would evolve. How would these dedicated men and women, all of whom I knew only from their official duties and their dark blue robes, experience such an evening? Would we all sit in serene silence and enjoy our roasted vegetables over a glass of lychee juice? What a surprise when that evening our plates were piled high with delicious meat, fish and vegetable satay and the wine flowed freely—at least for the guests.

When dusk started falling, we were treated to a *tai chi* workshop given by one of the masters. This created wonderful pictures of rather stiff Westerners manoeuvring themselves into uncomfortable positions as they tried to copy their limber Chinese teacher. When darkness had well and truly fallen, a karaoke sound set actually appeared—in good Chinese tradition. Visibly enjoying himself, Master Ren led the way and began to sing a Chinese hit, completely incomprehensible to us. In no time, the microphone passed from hand to hand generating spontaneous choirs and multi-lingual songs—at least, that's how it seemed to us. But the high point of the evening for me was undeniably the moment where Master Ren asked my granddaughter Stephanie to dance. A tall blonde lady and a short Chinese gentleman whirled across the cobbled square. What an unexpected feast and what an unexpected side to those otherwise so serious-looking masters!

The serious side got plenty of opportunity during the inauguration ceremony the next day. The faces of the monks and nuns performing the ceremony didn't show a single trace of the excesses of the previous evening. At least twice as many people as in 2005 were gathered on the square between the temple buildings. This time too, there was a coming and going of Chinese locals and tourists who watched at least part of the ceremony. After some opening remarks by the Vice President of the Shaanxi Daoist Association and the Director of the Shaanxi Religious Bureau, it was my turn to give a speech where I quoted Lao Zi on the conservation of nature.

Soon after, we again heard the singing, bells and drums of the nuns and monks, announcing the start of the ceremony. The table with yellow cloth was twice as big this time, the amount of fruit on the plates offered to the three gods of Taibai Shan appeared to have multiplied miraculously, and this time there were eight masters on both sides of the rug that covered the ground. Their robes were bright red and orange, decorated with yin-yang symbols, trigrams and Daoist symbols that seemed to be a cross between snakes and branches. Again, we could see and hear how the masters used their singing, rituals and music to invoke the gods who would then bless and safeguard the temple and the mountain. This time the rug on the ground was covered by a second rug depicting the *bagua* (the eight trigrams that in Daoist cosmology represent the fundamental principles of reality: water, fire, heaven, earth, wind, thunder, mountain, lake). Somewhere during the extensive ceremony, the master who was leading the ritual went on to a kind of dance across the trigrams. Martin explained that this created a link between heaven and earth.

Just as suddenly as it had started, the singing stopped about two hours later, marking the end of the ceremony. My family were given the opportunity to burn incense and place the sticks in the incense burner. I thought of my daughter Anneke; I thought of the marvellous journey that had brought me here to take part in this project; I thought of the tumultuous rediscovery that the age-old tradition of Daoism was going through. I thought of Guan Yin.

The Path to Taibai Shan Tiejia Daoist Ecology Temple

He Xiaoxin

The general idea was clear when ARC and WWF China launched a joint project in 2004: to restore an old Daoist temple and develop a training and exhibition centre on Daoism and ecology on Taibai Shan. The temple would be built as a model of eco-architecture using traditional, sustainable, local materials and it would engage local suppliers and builders. The training centre would be the springboard for spreading ecological awareness amongst Daoist temples nationwide. Together with a WWF China eco-lodge built earlier, the site could become a place for eco-tourism as well. The project would be executed in close collaboration with the local Louguan Tai Daoist Temple.

The realisation of the idea was a different story altogether. First of all, we had to obtain planning permission from the local authority. Fortunately, a deal was clinched within a few months. An agreement between ARC, the local authority and Louguan Tai Daoist Temple was signed in November 2004.

Designing the Temple

Next was the design stage. As a scholar specialised in Chinese traditional architecture, I provided some ideas. The temple should be in traditional style, e.g. in the form of a symmetric courtyard enclosed by walls. This was typical of traditional Daoist temples. Since I understood it would be hard to find builders skilled in a style true to the Ming Dynasty or earlier periods, I suggested the style of the Qing Dynasty. In the traditional, symmetric style, main halls or shrines are set up on a central axis, with other buildings that served Daoist religious functions positioned on the two sides. Living quarters, dining hall and other annexes are located at the back or on the side of the complex. Since our site was fairly small, a simplified version was proposed: a symmetric courtyard enclosed by walls but with all religious structures and functions—e.g. divine hall, altar, space to read scriptures or practise asceticism—put into one major hall on the axis. The same axis would also support another smaller-sized gate hall. This would house the ecology training and exhibition centre.

Inspired by the Daoist notion of living in harmony with nature, I felt the temple should not be surrounded by any man-made wall but by naturally grown bushes, shrubs and trees. This would set an excellent example for the rebuild or new-build of other Daoist temples in China. Furthermore, I suggested using local building methods and materials such as local pine and a basic structure made from wood.

Theory versus Practice

ARC's representative in China at that time, Zhao Xiaomin, discussed the initial ideas with the local authority and three local architects specialised in traditional Chinese architecture. He invited the architects to prepare a preliminary design. The winning design indeed showed a major hall which would be used as a traditional shrine and a gate hall that would serve as an exhibition and training centre. ARC, with funding from EMF's Allerd Stikker, would assist the local authority to rebuild these two halls. The local authority would then complete the remaining work.

But the design did not exactly follow our initial idea: it showed brick walls instead of ecologically-friendly shrubs. The architect and Xiaomin considered a temple without solid walls unsafe and thought shrubby walls would look rather shabby.

So we approved the preliminary design, albeit with some doubt, and followed it up with a more detailed design. We found a local builder

skilled in this kind of construction, and work on the major hall could begin. The expected completion date was the end of September 2005 and ARC was already planning the inaugural celebration and accompanying ecology workshops.

Brick by Brick

But, following an almost universal rule in the construction world, the building works failed to keep up with schedules. And by November 2005, nothing had been done, not even the foundation work of the major shrine. So ARC put me on a plane to China to talk to the stakeholders and see what was going on. I was a senior project manager after all.

My husband accompanied me on the trip and together we visited the construction workshop near the site. When we arrived, the builder showed us a wooden structure, explaining confidently that this was the frame of the main hall. My husband, a trained architect, looked at the beams and shook his head: this was not the structure of a traditional temple. The builder turned red with anger and insisted this was most definitely the Taibai Shan temple project. No, we argued, the shape and size were just wrong. So he hurried off to an assistant and came back apologising profusely: our temple was in one of his other workshops. Not wanting to embarrass him any further, we simply made sure he would do his utmost for us and left. Had Xiaomin not signed the contract, we might well have gone straight to the next builder. But at least we could rest assured he was reputed to be the best in the area.

Of all my meetings with the stakeholders, the discussion with Master Ren, the abbot of Louguan Tai Daoist Temple, was the most productive. Master Ren was in charge of the construction and management of the Taibai Shan temple and agreed to add 'ecology' to the temple's original name, officially turning it into Taibai Shan Tiejia Daoist Ecology Temple. He also agreed to rebuild the temple without a man-made brick wall and confirmed it would be safe. As a Daoist master, he very much appreciated the idea of harmonising the temple with its surroundings. We both agreed that the temple should harness this lost Daoist wisdom in order to kindle ecological awareness. Furthermore, Master Ren pointed out that it was against Daoist tradition to use the gate hall as an exhibition and training centre. His solution was to make a trade-off: we could have some unconventional features in our design but we should follow tradition as much as possible. I couldn't agree more. So in exchange for the shrub wall we gave up the idea of the gate hall for the training centre. We did of course need an alternative. One option was to add a structure on the west side, but this would destroy the symmetry of the whole layout. To be sure, there was a building on the east side, namely the run-down clandestine hall that the local people had built in the early 1990s. But it had not been built properly and was to be taken down in the near future, leaving an asymmetric whole.

At least so we thought. Master Ren explained that the existing east hall was crucial, providing accommodation for two or three resident Daoist masters and some pilgrims visiting Taibai Shan. So even if the old building were demolished, a new building on the east side would be required. This was indeed good news. A west hall housing an exhibition and training centre would actually maintain the overall symmetry of the courtyard. We agreed it was a brilliant plan, and so the construction of the major shrine and a west hall became the first phase. Local people would be responsible for demolishing and rebuilding the east hall.

Master Ren also suggested that such a small temple didn't need a gate hall. A small gate built of natural materials like rattan would be fine. A humble gate together with the surrounding bush-and-shrub wall would make the whole temple naturally integrated with the mountains and trees around it.

The visit may have been fruitful but the work was slow, partly because of poor weather. Phase 1 was eventually completed in spring 2007 with a wonderful ceremony to inaugurate the Daoist Ecology Temple Alliance.

Looking Back

The major shrine and west hall have now been built in the proper way with local pinewood, and the shrub wall blends in beautifully with the temple surroundings. I am pleased with the result.

I might have been even more pleased if the west hall hadn't been moved east by five or six yards, disturbing the symmetry of the courtyard and making it smaller than planned. I wasn't able to monitor the building works and, when I discovered the change, it was too late. This is my main regret and an important lesson learnt.

As yet, the existing eastern hall has not been rebuilt and the gate has not been erected. Perhaps it's too early to judge the whole layout. But what we do know is that the Daoist Ecology Temple has made pioneering contributions to the Daoist movement on conservation in China. The Qinling Declaration of 2006, which was drafted in an ecology workshop practically in this very temple, calls on people to protect the environment. The declaration has been carved in a stone near the temple as a solid reminder for pilgrims and visitors to protect the area and to travel green.

Be a channel for the energies here—

weave them in a true and practical way

so they can link up with the Dao

and become one again.

Chapter 28 of the Dao De Jing

4

The Birth of an Alliance

Daoist Temples Protecting Nature

The Daoist Ecology Temple on Taibai Shan was the first Daoist temple in China that was built and run entirely along ecological lines. It enjoyed widespread support ranging from an enthusiastic Master Ren to provincial government and from the China Daoist Association to the government in Beijing. The temple was an invaluable showpiece of what these parties could achieve together with ARC, that foreign body with its focus on religion and conservation. These were not exactly priority issues of the Chinese state. Xiaoxin told me later that the temple paved the way for all subsequent ARC activities in China. In this country, she explained, people are not interested in fancy plans or lofty promises but in concrete results. If you want to be taken seriously, you need to deliver. And that's precisely what ARC had done there. That's why it was able to contribute so successfully to restoring one of the most important pillars of Chinese culture.

It was of course not only the physical temple that mattered, but also what happened in and around the Education Centre. Together with the temple, the Education Centre aimed to put on the map the ecological principles so deeply anchored in the Daoist view of the world, thus creating ecological awareness in Daoist communities and ultimately far beyond. To achieve this goal, ARC had developed an ingenious and effective strategy that could be tailored to every country and every culture. The main idea was that ARC should inspire and facilitate. But religious groups should be at the helm themselves so they could chart and steer their own course towards a sustainable society. The trick was to start with religious leaders who had the commitment and outreach to turn ideas into concrete goals and actions. These could then be rolled out as full-scale programmes throughout the target region. In practice, this often meant that intentions would be formalised on a small scale in declarations and statements, and then applied on a wider scale. ARC's role would be to select key moments to celebrate achievements in full view of the press, inspiring other parties with a sense of urgency and desire to join up.

This strategy proved very useful in ARC's Daoism project. In China, ARC had found a most enthusiastic supporter in Master Ren. In the UK, Xiaoxin pulled the strings gently but firmly in her own personal but very successful way. Everyone at ARC knows the conversations between Xiaoxin and Martin whenever he came up with a new idea. She would invariably protest that such a plan was not feasible to which Martin then boldly responded that it would work. In fact, he argued, everything had practically been arranged. Without fail, Xiaoxin would get an almost impossible job done and with resounding success. As a typical example, Martin asked her one day to develop some information panels for the Education Centre. The panels had to display the ecological principles underlying the temple. They also had to incorporate the role of nature within Daoist philosophy. With a few suggestions and pointers on Martin's part, Xiaoxin took up the challenge. Within the agreed time, she unveiled some magnificent panels that to this very day give the temple its green face and spread the message of sustainability year-round. This, and other initiatives, enabled the Taibai Shan project to grow into an example not only for Daoists elsewhere in China, but also for the Buddhists and Confucianists later on—and not only in China, but also beyond.

The Ecology Temple together with Education Centre was intended to be a centre of expertise and education from the very outset. The educational aspect had been factored in at the 'birth' of the temple. The temple's inauguration ceremony, for instance, was going to be accompanied by a proper training programme. This would give participating monks and nuns concrete guidelines guaranteeing that sustainability would be anchored into their temples. The land that would ultimately carry the temple was inaugurated in 2005. This came a bit too soon for a training programme. But for the ceremony to be held the year after, Xiaoxin and Master Ren were very busy preparing a series of workshops about ecology and Daoism. The severe winter may have thrown a spanner into the construction works of the temple itself, but the training programme went ahead nonetheless.

So in July 2006, Martin, Xiaoxin and I travelled to Taibai Shan for a two-day workshop about Daoism and ecology. When we arrived, we were greeted by Master Ren once again, this time accompanied by a Chinese man with a strikingly modern hair cut. His clothing too told us he was not a religious Daoist. In his leather jacket over a trendy summer shirt, he could have come straight from the big city. It turned out that he was Professor Fan Guangchun, a lecturer and researcher at Shaanxi Academy of Social Science and specialised in Daoism. He was on the programme as one of the speakers and had been involved in structuring the programme. He also appeared to be a good friend of Master Ren, and of the inseparable variety because I think I always saw them together from then on. Some years later, Xiaoxin told me that Shaanxi Academy was one of the few research institutes that had such an extensive programme of research on Daoism. Moreover, Professor Fan's friendship with Master Ren put him in an unusual position. He had one foot in the theoretical world of academia and the other in the world of actual religious practice—a unique combination, in her opinion. We chatted for a bit over a cup of tea and then settled into the eco-lodge, a familiar place by now. On that same site, the workshops would be held in a meeting room next to a kind of canteen. It was a plain and simple room. I realised that any inspiration would ultimately have to come from the participants themselves. We would learn more the next day.

About twenty-five people were gathered in the room. Fourteen monks and nuns from ten different Daoist temples in Shaanxi and neighbouring Gansu province were sitting there alongside representatives of surrounding nature reserves, local conservation organisations and governments. The press was represented by the Development of Western China Magazine. This underscored once more the economic significance of the temple, one of the reasons after all why the provincial government supported the project. In terms of the audience, the workshop set-up was again a clever example of strategic networking. All regional, sectoral and national players of any import had been invited and were represented. In good Chinese tradition, the day began with opening speeches by organisers and dignitaries from various levels of government. Martin and I also had the honour of saying a few words.

The programme itself then got off to a flying start under the leadership of Xiaoxin and Master Ren. What happened in the next two days more or less passed me by because I don't speak Chinese. But I do know that, thanks to Xiaoxin and Master Ren, the process ultimately exceeded our expectations with the signing of a declaration and the establishment of the Daoist Ecology Temple Alliance. Here were the cornerstones of a solid institutional structure that would allow the message of sustainability to be disseminated on an ongoing basis. It was a great achievement because the final text of the declaration had not been prepared in advance but had to be drafted on the spot. The idea was that the presentations and workshops would initiate discussion. The final outcome would be a declaration setting out agreements and intentions, a basic document for participants to fall back on and to flesh out. It would be called the Qinling Declaration after the Qinling mountain range, home to the sacred mountain Taibai Shan and to the temples housing the monks and nuns who would attach their names to the declaration.

The speakers delivered the input for the discussions that laid the foundation of the Qinling Declaration. Professor Fan, for example, told us about his research into conservation activities by Daoist temples in north-west China. Master Ren described his personal rediscovery of the role of Daoist tradition in nature conservation. Peter Zhao talked about ARC's project to survey the sacred mountains and improve the protection of the region, pointing out the need for collaboration with local nature reserves. Xiaoxin gave a stimulating presentation, urging the fourteen monks and nuns to assess the sustainability of their temple management. This would then serve as a benchmark against which they could measure future improvements.

The ideas, brainstorming and feedback of the first day supplied the input for the draft text of the declaration. Working late into the evening, Xiaoxin, Master Ren and Professor Fan fine-tuned the words to create a declaration that every participant would be able to identify with. It would provide them with concrete actions to get their own temples onto the path of sustainability and spread the message. The story goes that Xiaoxin kept her drafting partners awake until the last full-stop was in the right spot. She later confided to me that these are precisely the situations where she comes into her own: grass-root-level projects that lead to concrete results and can be put into practice. Rather than using up energy, she said, it created energy.

The draft text was food for further discussion and amendment the next day, and at the end of that day, on 26 July, fourteen monks and nuns put their signatures to the Qinling Declaration. With the newly established Daoist Ecology Temple Alliance as a basis, they pledged to incorporate six Key Action Points into the construction, management and religious practice of their own temples—all in all, a wonderful moment because the centre of expertise and education had borne its first fruit even before the walls of the temple complex had been erected.

The Qinling Declaration meant a breakthrough, in Martin's opinion. For the first time since the Daoists had entered ARC with the Ecology Statement of 1995, a concrete follow-up step had been taken that fit in seamlessly with the Daoist view of the world. It was moreover anchored in an organisational structure. The Temple Alliance would make it easier to help and monitor one another and to expand the network. The first results and experiences would be discussed in a follow-up workshop planned for the next year.

The train had been put in motion with the Daoists themselves in the driver's seat, in perfect sync with ARC's vision. Here was marginal action at its best. I remember sitting outside the restaurant on the square sometime that weekend, having a beer with Martin. We noted with satisfaction that everything was going well. We were superfluous at that moment. The programme was in the capable hands of Xiaoxin and Master Ren. Our first meeting over dinner in 2002, the many conversations that followed, our shared fascination for Daoism—it was all falling into place.

I was also beginning to understand why Chinese people saw sacredness in the awe-inspiring mountains surrounding them, the place where heaven and earth touch, where according to Daoist tradition humanity should fulfil its task of guarding the balance between heaven and earth. It was gratifying to think that this task had now morphed into a concrete Daoist Ecology Temple and Education Centre and that its sponsors, in turn, had penned an early work, the Qinling Declaration, even before the temple itself was officially inaugurated.

The physical temple may have taken another year, but in 2007, the time had finally come. We again made the journey to Taibai Shan, this time to attend its inauguration. Xiaoxin and Master Ren had compiled a programme covering several days, following a familiar formula. 'Taking Care of Nature: Building up the Daoist Ecology Temple by our own hands' was a follow-up to the 2006 workshops. The programme would allow ample opportunity to discuss outcomes and experiences with the six items from the Qinling Declaration and to look ahead to the future.

In the space of a year, the original group had grown to eighteen monks and nuns from just as many temples. This was the maximum capacity of the meeting room by the eco-lodge, which would accommodate some of the activities. The discussions were considerably more lively than in 2006. Everyone was particularly willing to share experiences and knowledge. On top of this, the original participants had set to work with great enterprise and drive in order to make their temples more sustainable. It turned out that the abbots and abbesses had got going immediately with sun panels, water recycling and eco-friendly incense sticks. In the area of water and sanitation, too, close alliances between local communities and temples had sprung up everywhere.

Perhaps symbolic of the participants' zest and the success of their new path towards sustainability was the adoption of Lao Zi, the author of the Dao De Jing himself, as the Daoist god of Ecological Protection. It added an explicit link between Daoism and nature conservation. The eighteen participants also agreed to audit the ecological footprint of their temples using a questionnaire they had compiled during the workshops. This was how the path to sustainability would be clearly documented so that the steps to sustainability could be monitored.

Although 2007 featured a much larger touring party and a busy itinerary, I made sure to free up some time to enjoy Taibai Shan and the special temple. It helped me to find peace and calm, to feel reconnected with nature, humanity, the universe and eternity. I found peace and calm sitting on a rock by the water, just a mountain stream in the dry season, but a wildly swirling river during the monsoon. And I found it in the temple, resting with my eyes closed in the here and now and, at the same time, in the most unexpected and remote corners of my mind. Sometimes I was joined by pilgrims or visitors to the temple. They were looking for a moment of contemplation or an appeal straight to the gods. They would burn incense sticks to convey a message to the realm of the gods.

What I remember more than anything is a particular day when I visited the temple and it was empty. But just as I sat down, my world of silence was gently disturbed by the soft tinkling of a bell. I looked up and an older Chinese man of slight build had suddenly appeared. I asked him, with clarifying gestures, what the bell was for. He replied in deadly earnest that he had seen me coming and it was his task to warn the gods when there were people about, just in case they had dozed off in the serenity of the temple. So the Taibai Shan temple housed three unionised gods who worked in shifts and also quite happily had a kip during their shift. One thing's for sure: the Daoists have a good sense of humour.

And this, Martin says, is precisely the strength of Daoism: humour and perspective. You may think you know something and can take it for granted. And then it's ruthlessly called into question, but always with a touch of humour. Daoism puts the deepest philosophical thoughts into perspective with an element of jest. Here, Martin likes to cite the Zhuang Zi, his favourite Daoist text. The stories, sometimes in their very elusiveness, take you to the essence of the Daoist way of life. The 'Happiness of Fish', for example, is a story where Zhuang Zi and his best friend Hui Zi are once again in a heated discussion. It's a story where logic appears too clever for its own good:

Zhuang Zi and Hui Zi were strolling along the dam of the Hao Waterfall when Zhuang Zi said: See how the minnows come out and dart around where they please! That's what fish really enjoy!
Hui Zi: You're not a fish—how do you know what fish enjoy?
Zhuang Zi: You're not me, so how do you know I don't know what fish enjoy?
Hui Zi: I'm not you, so I certainly don't know what you know. On the other hand, you're certainly not a fish—so that still proves you don't know what fish enjoy!
Zhuang Zi: Let's go back to your original question, please. You asked me how I know what fish enjoy—so you already knew I knew it when you asked the question. I know it by standing here beside the Hao.

Light-hearted and amusing, these stories are brain-teasers. They disengage from everything that smacks of absolute truth. They dismantle the pigeonholes that we like to use for the seemingly neat arrangement of our everyday lives. In any event, this age-old, razor-sharp way of thinking had again acquired a face on Taibai Shan with the erection of the Daoist Ecology Temple and Education Centre. It was a modest contribution to the regrowth of one of the key roots of Chinese culture and to a renewed ecological awareness in that immense country, where the prevailing political mantra of economic growth had seriously upset the balance between economy and ecology.

In 2008, the third series of workshops was held by the Daoist Ecology Temple Alliance, again in collaboration with ARC. This time, the people who attended had outgrown the familiar eco-lodge once and for all. As many as sixty-nine monks and nuns from the entire country joined 120 government officials in Jurong. There was a special significance to this venue. Jurong lies at the foot of Mao Shan, one of the most important sacred mountains in Daoist tradition. Furthermore, Master Yang, the abbot of the Mao Shan Temple, was one of the driving forces behind the conference alongside Master Ren. I remember our taxi arriving in Jurong and stopping in front of a grand, brand-new hotel. The façade was almost completely hidden by colourful banners announcing the meeting: Dao follows Nature—The China Daoist Ecology Temple Forum. I saw the yin-yang symbol flowing into the web of life on one side and morphing into a sprig of budding leaves on the other side. It had been designed for the occasion but would blossom into the official logo of the Daoist Ecology Temple Alliance. In a flash, I saw how we had begun three years earlier with the first workshops in a rather dreary room near the eco-lodge by the square where we had enjoyed an unexpected barbecue and karaoke evening. In the next few days, one of the conference rooms would be packed with Daoist monks and nuns and representatives from a variety of organisations. They had come together to exchange ideas and experiences and were united in their goal of building and promoting the natural alliance between Daoism and ecology. And the sound of this gathering could be heard not only in China but further afield.

In previous years, ARC had entered a partnership with the United Nations Development Programme (UNDP). The idea was to help religious groups develop plans for the future so they could translate their sustainability goals into medium and long-term plans. These were Seven-Year Plans which would ensure that future generations would also safeguard the liveability of the environment. To achieve this, ARC and UNDP had already spent some time putting together a joint handbook, the *Guide to Creating Seven-Year Plans*. The Chinese Daoists were one of the first religious groups worldwide to start putting this guide into practice. In their case, it would be an Eight-Year Plan for the simple reason that eight is a lucky number in Daoism.

UNDP was represented by Deputy Director Olav Kjørven, an enthusiastic Norwegian whose personal efforts had resulted in UNDP's active involvement. This had not been easy. The UN was another organisation that didn't exactly rank religious groups as their preferred partners. Despite considerable internal resistance, Kjørven had success-fully managed to tie the religions into the development goals of the UN. He made no secret of his personal involvement and in an inspirational speech he said he was truly impressed by the wisdom of Daoism. In his opinion, this thousands-of-years-old tradition could be of great help to the sixty-year old UN in its own work. He argued that the notion of yin and yang, as it applies to humanity, drove home more clearly than any other religion the ecological challenges facing the world.

The UNDP spotlight also facilitated a comeback by the World Wide Fund for Nature (WWF). There was an attractive-looking, comprehensive conference booklet with the logo of the WWF as one of the sponsors. It appeared that this nature conservation body was also starting to shake off its fear of collaborating with religion.

In any event, these international organisations witnessed how a draft Eight-Year Plan was drawn up in no time and again under the impassioned leadership of Xiaoxin and Master Ren. The draft would have to be approved by the China Daoist Association (CDA)—a formal-ity, it was rumoured, if only because many local CDA representatives were involved in the plan. This time, Xiaoxin had received help from Claudia He, a young intelligent Chinese student who is gradually taking over Xiaoxin's role as ARC's China Programme Manager. Like Xiaoxin, Claudia's friendliness and kindness conceal a high-spirited woman who knows the ropes. With her broad American accent, she put in a marathon effort translating speeches, sessions and conversations.

The Ancient Green Revolution of Daoism

Professor Fan Guangchun

In 1966, when Fan Guangchun was fourteen, the Cultural Revolution broke out. He swiftly became the leader of the local Red Guard gang. At a time like that, it was impossible to keep yourself out of the swirling political storm. If you didn't go against the others, others would go against you.

They decided to follow Mao's edict to 'destroy the old' so they marched 20 miles from their hometown of Hanwang village to a famous Daoist mountain temple. There, directed by him, they destroyed all the statues. He had no idea who these gods were or what Daoism was about. It was just their job to strike hard and so they did.

When he was eighteen, he was sent to work in the countryside near Hanwang village as part of the drive to make intellectuals do manual labour. No help was given, so for three years he found sanctuary in a deserted Daoist temple, where he was surrounded by Daoist imagery. Later, he befriended the old Daoist monk who had been forced out of the temple during the Cultural Revolution. The monk taught him a lot about the different gods in the temple and about basic Daoism.

Years later, as a rising scholar of the very Daoism he had helped to destroy, he wrote a book about the mountain temple. This created so much interest that many, many more visitors and pilgrims started to visit the temple. This meant more donations and as a result the temple was restored. Strange to say, he is now known there as 'the man who destroyed the temple and the man who restored it'.

Professor Fan Guangchun is a senior research fellow and Director of the Daoist Studies Centre at the Shaanxi Academy of Social Sciences. He comments on the ecological dimension of Daoism.

In a time of global climate crisis, we tend to look for new, sustainable ways to connect and reconnect with the environment we live in. Daoism provides a valuable framework for a sustainable way of living for humankind. With justification, one could call the teachings of Lao Zi a 2,500-

year-old Greenpeace Declaration.

We can distinguish two different views on how humankind should understand the environment we live in. One is anthropocentric, considering humankind the central, most significant species on the planet. The other is non-anthropocentric, considering humankind equal to other species. The first advocate in China of non-anthropocentrism is Lao Zi. As early as 2,500 years ago, he promoted this view in the Dao De Jing. In this book, he described the relationship between Dao and life and pointed out that the rule of nature is the fundamental principle all human behaviour should be based on. We should treat nature with respect and awe, should not act recklessly and should not conduct warfare.

Most importantly, we should keep and preserve 'the three treasures'. The first of these is *compassion*: we need to have love for ourselves, for others and for nature. The second treasure is *moderation*: we need to live in simplicity, to avoid abusing power and material goods and to apply restraint when extracting resources. The third treasure is *humility*: we should not put ourselves before others and we should not pursue profit at the expense of others. To achieve a way of life in keeping with Daoist principles, Lao Zi repeatedly told people to practise abstinence, to be content and to avoid selfish plunder.

Daoist Precepts

The general guideline for the creation of a Daoist ethos is 'The Dao of the immortals treasures life and it provides infinite salvation.' This principle is reflected in the Daoist precepts, which emphasise our duty to preserve nature. Various Daoist classics have explicitly asked people to protect insects, plants, animals, mountains and rivers, and to avoid killing without very good reason. Among the Daoist precepts, there are many related to conservation, such as:

• *One should not kill any living being*
• *One should not burn (the vegetation of) uncultivated or cultivated fields, nor of mountains and forests*
• *One should not wantonly fell trees*
• *One should not wantonly pick herbs or flowers*
• *One should not throw poisonous substances into lakes, rivers, and seas*
• *One should not wantonly dig holes in the ground and thereby destroy the earth*
• *One should not dry up wet marshes*
• *One should not stamp on animals*
• *One should not watch animals mate*
• *One should not fish or hunt and thereby harm and kill living beings*
• *One should not in winter dig up hibernating animals and insects*
• *One should not wantonly climb trees to look for nests and destroy eggs*
• *One should not use cages to trap birds and (other) animals*
• *One should not light fires in*

the plains
- *One should not bring any beings and animals to extinction.*

Daoist Ecology Temple Alliance

The Daoists joined the Alliance of Religions and Conservation (ARC) with their ecological statement of 1995 and, since 2000, there has been a movement within the Chinese Daoist community to create Daoist ecology temples. ARC and the Dutch Ecological Management Foundation have actively participated in the process and attracted much-valued attention from the United Nations Development Programme.

The director of UNDP at that time, Dr Olav Kjørven, delivered a presentation at the Mao Shan Daoist Conservation Forum. He spoke highly of Daoist conservation ideas, and pointed out that 'the sixty-year-old UN should learn conservation wisdoms from ancient Daoism', thus highlighting the role of conservation efforts by the Chinese Daoist community within the global conservation movement.

In recent years, the Daoist Ecology Temple Alliance (DETA) has promoted a way of life that can be characterised as:

1. **Environmentally friendly.** The alliance emphasises the proper management of two relationships:
a. The relationship between humanity and nature, including mountains, forests, plants, water, wild animals, birds, etc. Daoist temples should be able to live in harmony and peace with them.
b. The relationship between Daoist temples and neighbouring communities. The temples should have a reciprocal relationship with their neighbours, share their living space and avoid exploiting others.

2. **Low-carbon.** In order to 'live long and have clear visions at old age', Daoism has accumulated a wealth of life-cultivating practices. However, to apply these practices, it is important to live an appropriate lifestyle. DETA first and foremost asks people to follow the 'three treasures' as advocated by Lao Zi in the Dao De Jing. To put them into the reality of modern life, they can be roughly adapted into three restraints:
a. Restraint on our desires. This can help us maintain our inner peace.
b. Restraint on our diet. We cannot live without the necessary grains, vegetables and meat. But excessive eating and drinking and unclean food could induce many diseases. This can be seen in the saying 'Illness comes from the mouth'.
c. Restraint on our consumption. This points to two things, namely the consumption of material goods and the consumption of our bodily energy. In the modern world, we are often tempted to exhaustion: all-night playing and entertainment, high mental pressure, long working hours, etc. All such actions go against Daoist teachings on health preservation.

The lifestyle advocated by the three restraints goes hand in hand with the popularly promoted low-carbon lifestyle and can benefit our environment in multiple ways: a reduction in the consumption of grains, meat, vegetables and oil; a reduction in carbon emissions from the production, preservation, transportation and processing of food; and a reduction in waste and noise.

This is why, amongst other plans, we intend to reintroduce the traditional Daoist fast days of the first and fifteenth days of the Chinese month, when only vegetarian food can be eaten.

3. **Energy saving.** A lifestyle that preserves health also saves energy. With this lifestyle, we can learn to live simply, thus reducing our consumption of water, gas and other sources of energy to a minimum.

Neither she nor Xiaoxin went to bed before 3 am. Night after night, they tweaked the text of the Eight-Year Plan with admirable dedication. The final result was a document establishing a practical definition of an ecological Daoist temple. It set out what standards should be met by any construction plans, educational programmes and other activities warranting the designation 'ecological Daoist'.

The workshops were closed with a formal statement and, this time, it was called the Mao Shan Declaration, after the famous Daoist temple that was just a stone's throw away. Each one of the sixty-nine monks and nuns who had signed the declaration pledged to dedicate themselves to making their temples and environment more sustainable on the basis of Daoist principles and to spreading the Daoist ecological message.

With the international spotlight turned on, this was not unrealistic. The presence of Kjørven and UNDP had achieved something else: the Daoists in China had made the government take notice practically overnight. The fact that the international community, in the form of UNDP, was associating itself with a centuries-old, oft-maligned tradition was a tremendous boost for the Daoists. And my guess is that it explains why there were more government officials than monks and nuns at the conference.

In any case, the tide was clearly turning for Daoism in China. The days when the Daoists were too poor to mend the roof of their temple, as a shivering Martin had discovered in 1993, and the days when Daoism was dismissed as a backward superstition in respected circles, as I had experienced myself in Taiwan in 1989, seemed to be over once and for all. The Chinese government and Daoism had found each other in the common goal to tackle what were substantial ecological and social problems in China.

During the workshops leading to the Qinling Declaration, my thoughts had taken me back to Taiwan, where my fascination for Daoism had begun around twenty-five years earlier. What would be the state of the environment on the island? At the end of the 1980s, after all, it was heading at full speed for a major catastrophe. What would be the state of Daoist tradition? In 2006, it may have been practised much more openly than in mainland China but its ties with ecological awareness had been rejected especially in scientific circles. The only one way to find out was to revisit the country.

So at the end of the programme surrounding the Qinling Declaration, I went on a sentimental journey to Taiwan, and its capital Taipei, in particular. This is where I had first encountered Daoism and had set out on the first leg of my journey with ARC and the Daoists. When I arrived at the airport, I was greeted by a stroke of luck. Large and colourful banners announced a special exhibition in the celebrated National Palace Museum in Taipei on none other than Guan Yin. There she was again, this time to welcome me back to Taiwan.

The first thing that struck me in Taipei was that face masks no longer dotted the street scene. The air was much cleaner than twenty-five years earlier. And the water that criss-crossed the city via numerous canals and rivers no longer had such worrying colours. At first glance, Taiwan had made a successful U-turn and was now following a more environmentally aware route. Going by the streetscape, this had not stood in the way of economic growth or welfare. Construction and other economic activity were thriving; the roads were as busy as ever; buildings were clean and in good condition; and there was a great variety of shops. It was good to see with my own eyes how this island had found a solution to its environmental problems in a relatively short period. As far as I could make out, it had found a new balance between ecology and economy. And, of course, I was happy that the *Taiwan 2000 Report* had given a pivotal push.

High on my wish list was a visit to Taipei's Long Shan Temple, the place where I had met Guan Yin for the first time. Her kind face among those gods with the savage looks, a scene which had caught my eye instantly, was still etched on my mind. I climbed the steps of the temple complex, a colourful island wedged between the beige blocks of flats and crowded Taipei centre. Everything looked exactly as it had twenty-five years earlier: the building still well-maintained, the splendid woodcarvings all smooth and shiny, the gold and copper fixtures nicely polished. It was as busy as it had been—if not busier—but the enormous hall absorbed the crowd effortlessly. And there she stood in the hustle and bustle of a huge temple complex. She was surrounded by people who, in their worship of her, seemed to have lost all sense of time and space: the goddess who hears all the sounds of the world, just as elegant, just as serene, and just as imposing as she had been before. I could feel again why she had made such an impression all those years ago, and why she had seemed so close ever since. I stood there for a moment and together with her I listened.

Naturally, I also wanted to visit the Guan Yin exhibition in the National Palace Museum. The grandeur of the museum and splendid location against the green hills on the fringes of Taipei make it worth visiting in its own right. You feel yourself shrink into insignificance when you walk through the immense gate towards the magnificent entrance. The museum is one of the biggest in the world and hosts an extensive collection of artefacts and works of art from the 8,000-year-old history of China. The collection hails from the Forbidden City, which banned the last emperor Puyi in 1924. Almost immediately after, the Forbidden City, with its huge imperial legacy, was turned into a museum. During the volatile years of the Sino-Japanese War, the Second World War and then the Chinese Civil War, General Chiang Kai-shek tried to safeguard the collection by splitting it into several lots and moving these around the country. But in 1948, the conflict came too close for comfort. He decided to ship the artwork to Taiwan and was just in time to ferry some 22 per cent of the most valuable works across the Taiwan Strait. This is the basis of what is now in the National Palace Museum. The remainder of the collection is back in its original place, in the Forbidden City, but now redesigned as a museum.

The collection in the underground repositories of the museum in Taiwan easily matches the quality of the works exhibited above ground. The museum has no difficulty putting together the most fascinating and extensive exhibitions by rotating works from its own collection. And since hostilities between mainland China and Taiwan have quietened down in recent years, their respective museums now exchange works with some regularity. It's a vast collection that definitely deserves more than an afternoon's visit but I was there with a single goal. I wanted to see the Guan Yin exhibition.

And it was a veritable feast. Never had I come across such an overwhelming number of Guan Yin images. Excellent engravings competed for supremacy with superb statues in *blanc de chine*, that famous Chinese porcelain—image upon image in numerous colours and styles, in all conceivable materials and poses, from every historical period. But always with that enigmatic smile so characteristic of Guan Yin. It made me think of Martin, who had written a book about her.

He would have been able to identify exactly which image belonged to which period or artistic movement. I relished in the abundance of Guan Yin and, in the following years, have often studied the magnificent catalogue of this exhibition to check what I had actually seen.

During my first trips to Taiwan, the seeds were sown for what would later become *The Transformation Factor*. This book owes a great deal to my conversations with the Jesuit priest Yves Raguin, an authority on Teilhard de Chardin who had lectured on Daoism at the local Catholic university. It appeared that Yves Raguin had passed away in 1998 but I very much wanted to meet his successor, Jean Almire Lefeuvre SJ. Perhaps I was unconsciously hoping that this man shared Raguin's philosophy, namely that a religion should adapt to the local flavour. Perhaps he had also studied Daoism. In any event, I had the opportunity to meet him but that was all.

My trip down memory lane would not have been complete without a return to the Grand Hotel in Taipei. This is where I had invariably stayed on my earlier business trips. It seemed as if time had stood still, if only because there, in that enormous lobby in the exact same spot as twenty-five years earlier, I caught sight of an old acquaintance. This was Julie Lin, one of the stall keepers in the lobby with whom I had developed a special bond of friendship during my Taiwan period. In those years, she had stood out with her gentle manner and what seemed her happy acceptance of a daily routine in her little corner of a big hotel. I had spoken to her and she had clearly been surprised, and pleased as well, that a foreign businessman would notice her and single her out for a chat, even if the English was a challenge. Bit by bit, our conversations became a fixture on my travels to Taiwan. My picture of her grew more detailed. I learnt that she was married with one child, whose future was her reason for going out to work. Her clockwork existence gave her peace of mind even if other people might consider it a grind. And her dearest wish was to see the inside of one of the smart night clubs, which were generally off limits to locals. So I invited her for a night out to one of these clubs. Sipping her fizzy drink, she visibly enjoyed the bustling atmosphere that evening. I realised that our conversations were an oasis of calm and simplicity for me, away from the hectic negotiations which were my reason for visiting Taiwan.

On that day, twenty-five years later, we had a heart-warming reunion.

I told her what had brought me to Taiwan. She promptly invited me to join her and her brother, a taxi driver, on a tour of all the temples in the neighbourhood where Guan Yin was worshipped. These trips were particularly agreeable and I was amazed at the popularity of this goddess. But the high point for me was a visit to Julie's own place. There, against one of the sitting room walls, was an altar dedicated to Guan Yin. I now had a behind-the-scenes glimpse into the home of an ordinary family in Taipei and their religious practices—if in fact religion was the right term. When I asked Julie if her altar made her a Daoist—or perhaps a Buddhist—she gave me a look of blank incomprehension. Did she not understand my question or was she perhaps afraid to give an answer? At that moment, I didn't see I had asked her a question she couldn't possibly answer. What's more, she couldn't even relate to the question because in Chinese and Taiwanese religious practice there's no distinction between different faiths. Somewhere down history lane, all the religious movements that might have reached China from the various corners of the world had become so entangled with Daoism—with some justification considered the only religion indigenous to China—that the resulting 'folk religion' and accompanying rituals could no longer be untangled into its constituent parts. And what of it? What difference does it make where the deity you worship at home comes from? What difference does it make whether you ask a Buddhist monk to cure an ailment or a Daoist master to grant a wish? It puts a completely different complexion on our Western desire to pigeonhole reality. We want to simplify things but doesn't compartmentalisation sometimes cloud our view of the whole? Doesn't our drive to label everything perhaps create contradictions that are needlessly played off against each other as being irreconcilable?

I was being confronted by the practical reality of a philosophical notion that had occupied me for several decades and that I have set out in my book *Three Windows on Eternity*. This is the notion that compartmental thinking in our Western world may well have enabled immense technological advancement, but that very same urge to compartmentalise has meant that we are now approaching the limits of what we can understand and measure. We will never be able to see the whole, let alone understand it, as long as we think in terms of opposites. We will always have gaps in our knowledge as long as we are unwilling to allow the possibility of *experiencing* whenever we are *exploring*. In clinging to what is measurable, we will continue to be confronted with mysteries by the non-measurable meta world, a world that forms an integral part of our lives and of the universe.

And who embodies these imaginary, flimsy lines between labelled truths more clearly than our Daoist goddess, herself the Buddhist male *bodhisattva* Avalokitesvara who became a female Guan Yin?

Without trying,

nothing worthwhile can be achieved.

Without awareness,

nothing can be achieved either!

Chapter 16 of Confucian Classic, the Shang Shu

5

Nationwide Commitment

Spectacular Moves from the Top

Oddly enough, what I remember most from the 2008 Mao Shan conference is my arrival back in Amsterdam. I put down my suitcase, opened the door to the garden room and, as was my habit, glanced up at the statue of Guan Yin standing on a shelf on the wall by the door. Just over three feet high and with some of the paint flaking off, this wooden statue may not have deserved first prize for the best image of Guan Yin. But to me it was very special if only because of the way it had come into my possession. In 1993, the very same year my mother passed away, I came across a tiny advertisement in a Dutch alternative magazine called BRES: Guan Yin statue for sale. There were no details, no explanation, not even a phone number—just a postal address. I was intrigued and wrote a letter to the seller. A few days later, I drove to his home in Egmond, a Dutch seaside village. I saw Guan Yin and was instantly sold. It was exactly what I had been looking for all those years. Without batting an eyelid, I paid the full asking price, put her in the car and raced back to Amsterdam. Not until later did I discover that I had bought an authentic, antique 18th century statue from China. Even the flaking paint appeared to be authentic. It had probably been used for worship in a family home and now she was in my home observing my life from her strategic pedestal. I sometimes felt it was she who made me aware that the time was ripe for Daoism to return to China.

The Mao Shan gathering had shown that Daoism was rapidly returning to its earlier position in Chinese society. What had started as a modest grass-roots initiative at a Daoist community level in Taibai Shan had grown into a nationwide movement with support from the authorities. And what's more, the ever-present state was itself working hard to direct Daoism back to the very heart of Chinese society. It had given space to the Daoists who, together with ARC, had risen to the occasion and begun applying their time-honoured wisdoms to the ecological challenges facing modern China.

Not that it was a done deal because, from time immemorial, everything in Chinese society had been—and continues to be—the outcome of a delicate game between the state and the people. I don't know of any other country or region in the world where the organised political top and the organically grown bottom are so well developed. The political establishment plays a key role in society but, at the same time, the people have their own ways. And in this relationship, religion has always been an important lubricant, although in the last century in particular, this role almost led to its own destruction.

So on the one hand, China is a country of age-old, powerful dynasties whose emperors were considered holy from the Qin Dynasty (221–206 BCE) onwards. Their absolute power quite literally determined the daily lives of their subjects. The Chinese calendar, for instance, was seen as a divine revelation promulgated by the emperor, the Son of Heaven. It was based on secret, complex calculations and presented to the public under imperial authority during the Chinese New Year. In fact, every decree issued by the emperor was observed as an eternal law that could not be changed. The emperor after all ruled under a Mandate of Heaven. And although the political leaders of the Republic of China (1912–1949) and the People's Republic of China (1949–present) would never use the designation 'holy', their *de facto* power was no less absolute and far-reaching than that of the emperors. The high (or rather, low) point was undoubtedly the period under Mao Zedong. During the Great Leap Forward (1958–1962), roughly 36–43 million Chinese (the exact figures are still a subject of research) starved to death as a result of the completely unrealistic economic and agricultural policies implemented by the Great Helmsman, coinciding with particularly bad weather conditions. The mind boggles at such figures and the realisation why so many people lost their lives. Their political leader had greatly overestimated his ability to mould society and nature as well as his own infallibility. The people themselves were paralysed by a sense of duty, fear and ignorance, and couldn't help being subjected to the terrible madness. Another example of political power today is China's one-child policy to control population growth. It has been in effect since 1970 and prohibits Chinese couples from having more than one child. Although the law allows many exceptions and is increasingly the subject of debate, the average Westerner finds it hard to imagine the authorities reaching into the bedroom. In Western eyes, it's an unthinkable example of top-down intervention.

On the other hand, China is also a country where communities are governed by a close-knit micro culture that goes back hundreds of years and seems to be miles removed from central government. Here, society is held together by old traditions dating back to the shamanism practised well before the Common Era. Local shrines have been the centre of the community for as long as anyone can remember. Built in traditional style, they are managed by the local population, who use them during festivities and religious services. They also serve as community centres where local sports clubs, theatres, guilds and traditional physicians can meet and where senior citizens can go to discuss the welfare of the community. Everyone has his own guardian angel, altar and incense burner. These societies are linked via the so-called Division of Incense: every new club fills its incense burner with ashes from an existing club elsewhere with which they want to be affiliated. This has created a tight-knit social, cultural and economic network of individuals, families and communities linked across regions and the entire nation without any interference from the central government.

The world-renowned sinologist and Daoist authority Kristofer Schipper has written about this at great length in his books. I've got to know him personally and never fail to get genuine pleasure from his almost bottomless pit of knowledge and experience of China and Taiwan. On this island, where I also became captivated by Daoism, he was the first Westerner to be ordained as a Daoist master. Schipper is an expert on the local Daoist structures and traditions and maintains that these networks, which operate under the radar of central government, were the reason Daoism has never left China. It even outlived the Cultural Revolution despite Mao's attempts to eradicate religion. Outside the political limelight, Daoism's strong network survived the storm, gave solace in difficult times and provided Chinese culture with continuity. Martin couldn't agree more, his favourite one-liner being: dynasties may come, and dynasties may go, but the Daoists will always be climbing their mountains. These words gave him the inspiration needed to carry out ARC's work and he always repeated them when asked how nature conservation could ever be served by collaboration with the world's faiths.

As for myself, I also learnt first-hand how much Daoism was part of the Chinese DNA. The Taiwanese officers, with their university backgrounds, knew their way around Daoist palm-reading rituals. And I saw it again many years later, in 2008, after the workshops in Taibai Shan. I had for a long time been wanting to visit Putuo Shan— an island south-east of Shanghai and dedicated to Guan Yin. Mount Putuo is one of the four sacred mountains in Chinese Buddhist tradition and is regarded as Guan Yin's *bodhimanda*, the place where she attained enlightenment. Xiaoxin and her husband, Jun, offered to accompany me on my trip. It appeared that the island was indeed covered with Guan Yin temples and statues and almost tasted too much of tourism and pilgrimage. But one thing I still remember vividly. I knew Xiaoxin and Jun, a successful architect, as down-to-earth professionals who weren't into religion. We were strolling past the many stands that flanked practically every temple and sold Buddhist paraphernalia. They each bought a chain with a Guan Yin pendant. It was not just as a fitting souvenir but actually to wear. And when they entered one of the temples, they kneeled three times before the Guan Yin altar as a matter of course. I would see the exact same thing in 2013 when I visited the Guan Yin altar in the famous White Cloud Temple in Beijing with Xiaoxin's successor Claudia. If I have ever come across a modern, intelligent young Chinese woman who fits perfectly into the current Chinese era of progress and development, then it has to be Claudia. I've never caught her showing any personal affinity for any religion but she also genuflected towards Guan Yin with great ease and skill.

To me, it was further confirmation that Schipper and Martin were right: a thin layer of secularism deposited by the state concealed a deeply rooted religious and cultural consciousness. The power of Chinese folk beliefs actually runs right through the history of the faiths in China. Daoism and Confucianism are seen as authentically Chinese but all other traditions that entered the country over the centuries acquired unmistakable Chinese features before they took root. I only need to look at the wooden statue of Guan Yin in my garden room. This was originally Avalokitesvara, a male Hindu deity. After crossing the border into China, he morphed into the female goddess Guan Yin, who then became immensely popular in Daoism and Chinese Buddhism. This final point shows another intriguing Chinese characteristic: officially, religious traditions might well have distinguishing labels but, at the individual or community level, there are no clear distinctions. I experienced this myself when I visited Julie Lin during my nostalgic trip to Taiwan in 2006. And Xiaoxin's and Claudia's unexpected Guan Yin worship illustrated that even the dividing line between atheism and religion is rather blurred. I once read that 40 per cent of government officials in China have a religious affiliation even though China is officially a communist country which by definition is non-religious and where civil servants are supposed to declare themselves atheists.

So when ARC joined the Chinese Daoists in 1995, it entered a very complex social arena. On one side of the field stood society looking for its own cultural identity at grass-roots level and trying to fend off the state intervention it distrusted so much. And on the other side stood the state, fearful of religion's uncontrollable mobilising force and keeping a heavy-duty boot in the door. For ARC, it was not exactly a picnic. It takes considerable diplomacy—especially for a foreign organisation—to navigate such forces and conquer a position. But with a good feel for the political set-up, knowledge of Chinese society and perfect timing, Martin and his team managed it in quick time. All I can say is that I have the greatest admiration for what they've achieved. And it's all the more admirable given that the first meeting with the long arm of the Chinese state was not entirely friendly. Martin experienced this first-hand when ARC was doing research into the biodiversity of the Daoist sacred mountains between 1996 and 1998. Martin lost count of how many times Peter Zhao and Tjalling Halbertsma had to be rescued from the hands of the police. The state let it be known it would have the last word on what happened in Chinese society.

And that wasn't all. The report that summarised the research was not an easy sell either. It showed that the places in the sacred mountains where religion was actively practised displayed a much healthier biodiversity than other places. Shortly after its publication, ARC was approached by UNESCO to help them examine the possibility of putting Hua Shan on the list of world heritage sites. For more than three thousand years, Hua Shan has been the most sacred of the Chinese mountains. It's the sacred mountain where, in Chinese folk tradition, humans originate and return after death. The Chinese state had ambitious plans to boost tourism to Hua Shan with the construction of a motorway, cable car and various tourist attractions. ARC presented UNESCO with the sacred mountain report, recommending that they should urge the Chinese state to reverse their plans and allow more space on the mountain for religious activity. UNESCO agreed but the Chinese government refused to consider it: religion was an anachronism and irrelevant to economic progress. There was a huge conflict, but in the commotion Martin and his team managed to exchange a place on the list of world heritage sites for a pledge that the Daoists would get back 124 temple sites confiscated during the Cultural Revolution. Furthermore, one of their own would be a member of the mountain management bureau and they could keep 10 per cent of the proceeds from ticket sales to help defray management costs. The deal was a tremendous breakthrough: a categorical 'no' to religious activity and a one-dimensional 'yes' to commercial tourism had given way to a compromise whereby the Daoists would get a seat at the negotiating table and their own source of income.

It was a clever piece of diplomacy that nevertheless had everyone on edge to the very last moment. Martin's tale about the lunch given to celebrate the deal is both legendary and hilarious. Chinese tradition dictates that an official state banquet always features several obligatory toasts with Maotai, the famous Chinese liquor whose alcohol content is not inconsiderable. After the third toast, Martin sighed to his interpreter that it was a good thing they were not in Russia. They would have had at least eight more rounds. Before he knew what was happening, his interpreter had shared this comment with his Chinese hosts. Now if anything can stir up the Chinese competitive spirit, then it's a comparison with Russia. What should have been the final toast suddenly appeared to have been a warm-up for what was to come. Martin did some quick thinking. Here he was with several ambitious Chinese officials who, instead of getting a tourist attraction, had been

saddled with an agreement involving an oft-reviled religious group—
not exactly a dream deal and a loss of face as well. What a piece of luck
if Martin got drunk and the deal fell through! Martin quickly passed
every glass that came his way to Norman Winter, the cameraman he
was travelling with to shoot a BBC series about China. It saved Martin's
face, the deal and Hua Shan, but all we know about poor Norman is that
he can't remember what happened the next two days. He didn't wake up
until Beijing airport, where he cheerfully told two fellow passengers
about the beauty of Hawaii.

ARC may have manoeuvred their way through vested interests with
skill and success but their position as the lynchpin between the Daoists
and the state wasn't established until the construction of the Taibai
Shan Daoist Ecology Temple. The political landscape on the side of
the state which ARC had to deal with is a complex as well as fascinating
example of Chinese pragmatism. Operating from the central government in Beijing, the State Administration of Religious Affairs (SARA)
controls everything that happens in the religious sphere. It seems a
hopeless contradiction that a state advocating atheism should actually
have a ministry for religious affairs. It seems even more ironic that
SARA's predecessor, the Religious Affairs Bureau (RAB), was set up in
1954 under Mao of all people, the communist leader who made history
as the destroyer in China of anything with religious overtones. And yet
it illustrates beautifully the creativity and pragmatism of the Chinese
in terms of adapting reality to a theoretical construct. Mao's attitude
towards religion was driven much more by crafty pragmatic, political
and strategic action than by dogma or principle. His communist vision
essentially considered religion irrelevant and he was not so much
concerned with destroying religion *per se* as with annihilating a force
that might turn against him. And conversely, he realised all too well
that he could harness religion to serve his own purposes.

The moral and ideological foundation of this pragmatic strategy lay
in Mao's differentiation between 'religion' and 'superstition'. Friendly
religious leaders enjoyed protection against Mao's army under the flag
of religion while religious traditions who identified with hostile groups
were persecuted under a host of categories covered by the umbrella of
superstition. To justify this distinction, Mao could simply turn to the
past: through the centuries, emperors had applied the same trick, using

religious differences to defend internecine battles; while leaders during the Chinese Republic maintained a ban on superstition to jumpstart China's modernisation. Mao could also take advantage of what was a very fine dividing line between religion and superstition. In China, indigenous religious practice (Buddhism, Confucianism and Daoism) often embraces shamanic rituals such as divination, fortune-telling, exorcism and sacrifice. And the numerous movements, cults and hybrids within these traditions clutter up the religious landscape even more. It was precisely this chaos that allowed Mao to draw the line as he saw fit.

The resulting uncertainty created an atmosphere of paranoia and fear amongst religious followers. Religious groups had an interest in being labelled as a religion by Mao, especially as victory by the Communist Party came closer. It could mean the difference between life and death. So here we have the origin of patriotic religious associations, the predecessors of today's official religious associations, which continue to enjoy state protection. The associations demanded a certain degree of organisation and, in practice, it meant that institutionalised convents, brotherhoods and religious orders were the ones to carve out a place for themselves. In other words, the organised replaced the organic, creating a religious landscape where an organised top was no longer in touch with organically grown religious communities.

This was particularly disadvantageous to the Daoists. Daoism, by its very nature, was rooted in local communities, where masters conducted rituals and services for local inhabitants. These people were just as likely to turn to other indigenous traditions like Buddhism and Confucianism, so the Daoists lacked a system of official registration and hence organisation. What's more, the Daoist structures were closely tied to the old political order under the feudal empire and resided mostly in rural areas. And this is exactly what Mao was aiming at: destruction of everything that savoured of feudalism and the old empire in a push from the countryside. For the Daoists, it meant that the age-old structures supporting religious practice were taken down. The monastic Quanzhen tradition was the only movement within Daoism with a modicum of organisation and thus in a position to take root in the new religious order. This explains why Daoist representation within the Chinese state apparatus is very incomplete and lopsided and why, more than any other religion, Daoism was forced to redefine its position, structure and role in society. It went through a period of deep crisis but of new opportunity as well.

After Mao took power in 1949, the religious system with its various categories was made permanent in the political structure of the new communist People's Republic of China. In 1954, the Religious Affairs Bureau was set up with the religious associations falling under it. In this set-up, RAB not only determined religious life but it could steer and infiltrate in order to reinforce the message of patriotism. The Cultural Revolution then ruthlessly attacked all forms of religion so that even the religious structure that had emerged in the previous decades had to take backstage. However, after Mao's death in 1976, his successor Deng Xiaoping inherited what was still an intact religious structure that could easily move back onstage. The distinction between religion and superstition is maintained even today. Religious recognition may no longer mean the difference between life and death but it does determine access to resources, like funding, freedom of movement and the likelihood of survival—although the persecuted Tibetan Buddhists, Muslim Uyghurs and Falun Gong practitioners are bound to feel the brutal side of the distinction.

In 1998, RAB was renamed the State Administration of Religious Affairs, whose task was to protect and help officially recognised faiths in their religious practice. For many generations, the five officially recognised religions had—and have—been Buddhism, Daoism, Islam, Protestantism and Catholicism. Confucianism is not on the list because it is not deemed a religion. Mao purged it of all religious elements, thus clearing the way for its incorporation as the official state philosophy— a status it has kept to the present day.

To grant 'protection' and 'assistance', SARA defined for itself a broad set of tasks, ranging from the registration of the clergy, temples and churches to the financial and general management of sacred places. Registration meant that the state also exercised strong influence on educational curricula and religious appointments. In these endeavours, SARA worked closely together with the associations of the five religions set up in the Mao era and earlier. These national associations in turn presided over an extensive network of provincial and local branches. With so many layers, the local colour very much determined how strictly central policy was implemented and enforced. Apart from the branches that monitored the everyday practices of the recognised religions, SARA had a division whose task was to examine policy as well as monitor and investigate 'folk' and 'new' religions like Judaism, Sufism and Baha'i.

It's not hard to see that such protection, assistance, monitoring and investigation could have a dark side, namely control and influence. Religion was tolerated but only if it operated within the state objectives of safeguarding social harmony and stymieing potentially subversive elements. From the very outset, the state's attempt to control and influence led to strong distrust amongst religious followers towards the state and even towards religious leaders and associations them-selves. The latter were after all just state appointments, or at best appointments approved by the state. It was up to religious leaders to perform the delicate task of striking a balance between loyalty to the state and representation of the rank and file, i.e. between an organised top and an organically grown bottom. In this sense, nothing changed when Mao departed.

Even so, there was an important difference thanks to the social and economic freedom under Deng Xiaoping's leadership. In the distinction between religion and superstition, the freedom afforded to religion no longer lay in the religious sphere but in the social domain. It became attractive to associate religious practices with tourism, health and science, to name a few examples. Temples became tourist attractions and health-preserving rituals previously labelled as superstitious could be given a new twist and regarded as medical practice or scientific research. Again, we see a clever example of Chinese pragmatism, creativity and resilience beyond the Western mentality of pigeonholing: it's hard to beat the Chinese when it comes to bending and massaging reality.

In this case, it was the much-maligned Daoism that benefited. It had to re-establish its bearings but without the old imperial structures. The way was in fact clear for a completely new and modern interpretation of timeless Daoist wisdoms. It turned out that issues like ecology, gender equality and traditional Chinese culture fit very naturally into a Daoist context. And the same was true of old traditions like *tai chi*, *qigong*, *feng shui*, as well as traditional Chinese medicine and methods for self-development. Revamped and rebranded, they put Daoism back on the map—and not only in China but far beyond. The other side of the same coin is that a period of religious flux tends to attract charlatans and might give way to commercialisation. We are unlikely to have seen or heard the last of scandals over confidence tricksters and the moral degradation of sacred places and traditions resulting from the pursuit of profit.

But one thing we do know: the centuries-old tradition of Daoism, which had lived on in the smallest communities and the hearts of the Chinese and survived the most trying times, was again showing its universal value and resilience. And this was starting to dawn on the Chinese government. ARC had clearly sensed it was in the air and had been instrumental in initiating an effective and sustainable link between ecology and Daoism. It was now 2006 and Martin was invited to a face-to-face meeting with several senior party officials. When he arrived, there were even some ministers. Such a heavyweight delegation made Martin think the worst but, to his surprise, an open and sincere conversation ensued. This historic meeting would have a huge impact, not only on Martin personally but also on the course of ARC's activities in China. Listen, the mighty gentlemen said, we are stuck with an enormous problem. Our one-child policy has created the most egocentric, materialistic generation ever. You can't find a country anywhere with such pampered children who are the centre of family life and their own universe. In a period of exponential welfare growth, the younger generation are focused exclusively on money and material things and don't really care about the ecological dangers we are facing. We have very few instruments to address these. In the past century, we have lost touch with our roots and our Chinese identity. We see only one way to restore that identity and inject some morality back into society, namely through religion. If there is a sense of solidarity and community, compassion and identity and non-consumerism anywhere in China, then it is in traditional Chinese religion. So we call on you to help us bring Daoism back to the heart of the Chinese and our society.

Upon hearing these words, Martin immediately realised the Chinese plea not only passed muster but swung open the door to ARC's mission of giving Daoism the latitude to reposition itself and shape its ecological message. And it was, of course, an incredible vote of confidence and recognition for the work Team Martin had done with the Chinese Daoists in the preceding years.

Mao Shan Qianyuan Daoist Temple

Abbess Yin

Abbess Yin Xinhui was born just before the Cultural Revolution broke out. She is a representative of a generation that experienced the atrocities of the Mao period and consciously chose to return to the roots of an old Chinese culture that had almost been washed away.

She is widely regarded as a master who advocates authentic Daoism. With the new religious freedom and under the influence of the state, temples and traditions often serve tourism and other commercial purposes without any concern for religious traditions. Abbess Yin openly opposes such commercialisation.

Nobody will forget her actions during the opening of the new Jade Emperor Temple on Yi Shan. The local authorities had invited her, as an expert on Daoist ritual, to take care of the opening ceremony. She agreed but point-blank refused to shorten the four-hour ceremony just because the government officials who were coming had to keep to a schedule. On the day itself, the ceremony was indeed interrupted for the official speeches, but the ritual attracted large crowds, including the spouses of the officials themselves. Of all things, the austere, authentic Daoist practices championed by Abbess Yin appear to be a huge commercial success.

Master Yin Xinhui is the abbess of the Mao Shan Qinyuan Daoist Temple. She talks about the history of the temple and temple life today.

Mao Shan Qianyuan Daoist Temple is one of the most famous Chinese grottos in history. The temple is surrounded by bamboos and pine trees, giving it a quiet and surreal atmosphere.

Many Daoist high monks and lay believers would retreat to this place to practise Dao. In the Qin Dynasty, a Daoist alchemist named Li Ming started practising here, and the place was called Lian Dan Yuan. It was here that, during the South-North Dynasty, the great Daoist Master Tao Hongjing built the Pagoda of Pine Wind. Following in the footsteps of previous high masters, Tao refused several times to serve in the court of Emperor Liang Wu, but the emperor nevertheless consulted him whenever a big decision needed to be made. People at that time called Tao 'the minister in the mountain'. In subsequent dynasties, the temple was extended and renamed many times. In the Yuan Dynasty (1271–1368), there were about eight hundred rooms in the temple and in the early years of the Republic, the temple saw its first abbess: Master Hui Xinbai.

On 6 October 1938, Japanese colonists burned down Mao Shan Qianyuan Temple, killing Abbess Hui Xinbai and eleven others. Not until 1993 did the government of Jintan County agree to rebuild and reopen the temple. With the support of both the Communist Party and the government and under the auspices of local communities, the temple was successfully rebuilt and expanded through the joint effort of all Daoist believers.

Female Daoists at Mao Shan Qianyuan

Under the aegis of our ancestral masters and with the trust and support of government and faith communities, I was put in charge of the restoration of Mao Shan Qianyuan Temple. Whereas it was a place traditionally housing male Daoists, it became a temple for female Daoists. The reconstruction was a task that required perseverance, hard work and sincere prayers; without these, it would have been impossible to rebuild a thousand-year-old temple in the middle of the wilderness.

We are lucky that today we live in a time of great national prosperity and strength. The government employs a liberal religious policy, but we had to organise funding ourselves. Qianyuan Temple is located in the heart of Mao Shan and is difficult to access. At the time of the rebuild, it had no power or running water. The few simple rooms were in bad shape and in need of repair. In August 1993, we rebuilt three rooms to host the three Gods of Purity, thereby reinstating a tradition that had been disrupted for fifty-five years.

In November 1993, I accepted seven female Daoists as my first students and led them to the road of a diligent practice of Dao. We sang prayers and performed rituals and blessings day and night and studied the Daoist teachings tirelessly. In the morning, we went up the mountains to collect firewood and stones, cultivated the fields to grow our own food and cleared wasteland. In order to raise funds for the rebuild, we went everywhere. We built altars and we warmly welcomed guests and travellers.

Mao Shan Qianyuan Daoist Temple is the only female Daoist temple in Jiangsu Province. At first, not many people knew about this temple, and even fewer people knew that the Mao Shan School of Daoism included female Daoists. Many people thought we were Buddhists. But in the past twenty years, the temple has recovered its former glory and the Great Dao once again shines because our female Daoists have worked hard, lived virtuously and learnt diligently, each abiding by Daoist precepts.

Today, Qianyuan Temple in Mao Shan covers a large area, connecting the Daoist Culture plaza and Golden Roof in a straight line. The whole temple is a splendid edifice in a serene atmosphere and beautiful environment. A friend wrote a poem to describe the beauty of the temple:

A place of purity
Decorated by heavenly cloud-covered
mountain wind
A blessed grotto in a wilderness
Surrounded by seas of bamboos
and waves of pine trees.

Female Daoists Re-establish Daoist Teachings

Dao is expressed through people. While it is important to rebuild Qianyuan Temple, it is more important to nurture the people. We school our own female Daoists and the masters preach to their own students. They learn together and make progress together. We also invite high masters to come and preach and send our youngest Daoists to study in other places. In this way, we have steadily cultivated a young group of female Daoists with a good education and a good understanding of Daoist practices. In 2012, we hosted the first Mao Shan Qianyuan Temple International Seminar on Jiang Nan Quanzhen School Daoism. At the seminar, we absorbed a good deal of history and advice on how to promote Daoism.

We are in the process of establishing Mao Shan Academy as a base for Daoist training and education. We are also setting up a Daoist library, hosting classes on Daoism for followers and believers, and organising charities and events to help the needy. We will continue with these initiatives to promote Daoism.

Preaching Dao and establishing Daoist virtues are traditionally the responsibility of all Daoists and important ways of practising and promoting Dao. The female Daoists in Mao Shan Qianyuan Temple work to improve the community around them and purify people's souls. We foster orphans, nurse the old, attempt to reduce poverty and carry out disaster relief. We protect the environment and treasure all living things. The female Daoists manifest the Great Dao and Daoist traditions.

Music is a part of Daoist rituals and ceremonies and it is very popular in our temple and local community. In 1995, we established a female Daoist orchestra. Since then, we have asked each Daoist to learn an instrument to promote Dao, acquire inner peace, cultivate health and help others through music. Our performers are well credited locally, nationwide and overseas for upholding the pure Dao. They are disciplined, dignified and simply splendid. Our Daoist orchestra has performed fifteen times in Singapore, six times in Taiwan, in Hong Kong and Macao and at major events in mainland China. In 2010, we successfully hosted the tenth Daoist Music Showcase in our temple, along with Taiwan Cihuitang Chinese Orchestra, Hong Kong Daoist Orchestra, the White Cloud Temple in Beijing, Shandong Lao Shan, Hubei Wudang Shan and Mao Shan.

Authentic Daoism in Practice

There is an old saying which reads 'in times of prosperity, people build temples'. Daoism developed along with Chinese society and a progressing human history and continues to do so. Over the years, Daoism has adjusted to a changing environment through the practices of great masters and it has demonstrated its flexibility and popularity.

Even so, historical disruption has meant that there are fewer young Daoists than before. In addition, Daoism has seemed slow to adapt to modern times, to the rapid developments and changing ways of thinking. Some Daoist temples have also been run poorly, causing a decline in popularity.

Since construction began at Mao Shan Qianyuan Temple, I have recognised these problems and decided to make a few adjustments to our traditional practices. With regard to management, I have decided that the temple should be run democratically instead of single-handedly. Daoists with virtues and talent will be elected to form the management core. All Daoists are required to follow closely the teachings of ancient masters and uphold Daoist principles. Their behaviour should reflect Daoist regulations and precepts at all times. Strict rules of accounting are applied and financial reports are updated on a monthly basis to make sure our finances are transparent. We have created archives and follow the principles of fair governance.

These changes have been very well received.

Mao Shan Qianyuan Daoist Temple is a place of serenity and tranquillity. The female Daoists follow their beliefs wholeheartedly and practise the pure Dao. They make sure Dao is their fundamental guiding principle and act to manifest the Great Dao. Their noble behaviour has helped establish virtues and contribute to our society. In May, the 102-year-old Master Zhang Zhishun from Zhongnan Mountain visited our temple. Feeling the gathering momentum of Daoism, he made the following wish: may the Great Dao spread from Mao Shan Qianyuan Temple.

I thought it was an impressive story and I wondered how a foreigner of all people had managed to manoeuvre himself into this position. China, after all, had a reputation for viewing any foreign meddling with great suspicion. Martin's explanation was just as logical as it was tragic. The wholesale marginalisation, ridicule and destruction of Daoism meant that by the end of the Cultural Revolution almost all temple artefacts had been lost and fewer than one thousand monks and nuns lived to tell the tale, although many were too traumatised and were simply wasting away. Almost all texts, liturgies and knowledge that had survived were in other countries. Furthermore, the new generation of Chinese no longer mastered the classical Chinese of ancient writings. And they weren't too interested anyway because Daoism was still seen as a backward superstition. The books on Daoism that were written in modern Chinese—mostly historical studies by academics—were not exactly unbiased: they had after all been produced under the supervision of the Communist Party, which still preached atheism. So was it any wonder that the authorities had to look across the border for original texts and information on Daoism. This is where Martin's translations of the Zhuang Zi and Dao De Jing came in. He had shown the requisite interest and knowledge—two essential qualities for anyone who wants to be taken seriously in China. Moreover, the construction of the Taibai Shan Ecology Education Centre and workshops were evidence that ARC could make a concrete contribution. I personally think the achievements also show the value of marginal action: ARC helps religions worldwide to consider and shape ecological awareness from within their own traditions. They don't prescribe but inspire. And the fact that ARC was no longer seen as interference from abroad, and was even respected and valued, is clear proof that Martin and his team had mastered the ins and outs of this strategy. ARC had shown it could manage with true integrity the trust it had gained from the state and from the Daoist community. It was the link between top and bottom and with justification.

This historic meeting demanded a concrete follow-up and Martin was of course more than willing to help. There was a plan on the table for a major international conference with the Daoists, and this time the express commitment from the state would have to be visible. Up to this point, workshops with the Daoists had been grass-roots initiatives by the Daoists with government officials as invitees. The roles were now reversed. SARA and CDA were in charge of organising the conference and the Daoist monks and nuns were part of the audience. When asked about the programme for the conference, Martin replied that ecology was an important theme, but he felt it would be better first to acknowledge that Daoism had something to offer and to show that the state would support it. After many years of suppressing and ridiculing Daoism, the government had to repair the damage if they wanted to appear credible. And it seemed no more than natural to go back to the principal text of Daoism, namely the Dao De Jing.

In the spring of 2007, Xian hosted an ambitious five-day International Dao De Jing Forum. For the first time in fifty years, the Chinese state was organising a conference on one of the most crucial texts from its own culture. About three hundred participants gathered together to hear and discuss how a view of the world going back many centuries could make a contribution to what was also the conference topic: constructing a harmonious world.

Unfortunately, I couldn't attend myself but Martin's and Xiaoxin's stories at the end of it all are legendary. If the Chinese government puts its weight behind anything at all, then it seems the sky's the limit. Just the opening ceremony by the gate in the old city wall was a grand spectacle, complete with ritual dance and music choreographed and composed by famous Chinese artists. It was broadcast live on Chinese TV and gave Martin the opportunity to present a message from Prince Philip before the entire nation showing his respect and appreciation for Daoism. Perhaps that silly superstition wasn't so silly after all. In any case, the event contributed to China's standing in the international arena.

For five whole days, dignitaries, experts and masters came and went. From an impressive podium, they paid extensive homage to Daoism and analysed China's problems. Martin and Xiaoxin were full of vivid stories and, with my own modest experience of Chinese conferences, I could picture it all. But the absolute high point was a speech by Liu Yandong, Vice-Chairman of the National Committee of the Chinese People's Political Consultative Conference (CPPCC), China's most important legislative body. This high-ranking party official, with her far-reaching authority and power in the CPPCC, plainly stated that the wisdoms in the Dao De Jing were invaluable for present-day China and that this ancient world view should return to the heart of Chinese society.

When I read an English translation of the speech afterwards I was pleased. In the late 1980s, I had witnessed in Taiwan how Daoism was being dismissed in political and scientific circles as a backward and even harmful superstition. Less than a quarter of a century later, a high-ranking party official spoke about the need to restore the Daoist roots of Chinese culture.

And the conference yielded another outcome that would be crucial to ARC's work in China. Martin told me he had been given an enormous hotel suite with a kitchen, posh seating area for visitors, and guest wing. At first, he was somewhat overwhelmed but then slowly understood it had been arranged that way on purpose. One after the other, Chinese delegations knocked on the door to talk to him about collaboration, initiatives, and yes, even English lessons! Martin had always wanted to remain in the background with ARC, as befitted ARC's strategy. But this was rather tricky for a 'most-honoured guest'. It was becoming ever clearer that Martin was turning into the face of a revived Daoism. It was another piece of evidence that he was regarded as an important partner by the state as well as the Daoists.

It also gave him the opportunity to present the highest SARA official with a proposal to formulate a multi-year plan with the Daoists. Together with UNDP, ARC had just put the final touches to the *Guide to Creating Seven-Year Plans*. Now the time had come to put the guide into practice. ARC received the green light to sit down with the Daoists. It was up to Xiaoxin to take up the gauntlet. As was the case during the Taibai Shan workshop in 2006, this meant knocking on the many doors of local and state officials. It meant talking with people, keeping them informed and negotiating who would contribute in which phase and how.

Along the way, some hairline cracks started to appear in the complex arena where ARC was liaising between the state and the Daoist community. The Daoist Ecology Temple Alliance, backed by ARC, was steadily gaining ground in their attempt to give the Daoists more elbow room. It was a particularly successful grass-roots movement—perhaps a little too successful for CDA's taste. It began to see the Daoist alliance as a fearsome competitor for its own role as captain and liaison between SARA and the Daoist community. In the run-up to the meeting in Mao Shan, Xiaoxin was often left standing in the cold outside the CDA offices as she tried to drum up interest in the Eight-Year Plan. And since all plans and initiatives for the Daoists—no matter how big or small—required approval from CDA, there was no escaping this organisation. The question was not whether to get approval from CDA but how.

It was a tough chapter in the ARC annals. Xiaoxin had to weigh the interests of Master Ren and fellow Master Yang of the Mao Shan Temple, local officials, and participating research institutes as well as those of SARA and CDA. Every contact and word chosen was carefully weighed and Xiaoxin must have talked herself hoarse. By pulling out all the stops, she finally managed to get CDA on board. With the 2007 opening ceremony of the Taibai Shan Temple and workshops, ARC and the Temple Alliance had shown they could really get results. And when UNDP suddenly arrived on the scene just before the Mao Shan meeting, CDA finally came round. With all the important players on board, ARC could pave the way for a successful conference in Mao Shan, where a first version of the Eight-Year Plan would be drafted. The Daoists identified six areas for special attention to help spread the ecological message in subsequent years, ranging from the sustainable management of land and buildings to education and from the promotion of an ecologically responsible way of life to more sustainable feast days and traditions.

Approval for the Eight-Year Plan from CDA headquarters was indeed just a formality in the end. It came in 2009 and the Daoists were ready to pay their respects at Windsor. Martin had chosen the 'birthplace' of ARC and the back garden of founding father HRH Prince Philip as a setting for the event. He wanted to turn the spotlight on the long-term plans of the nine religions that were affiliated with ARC. Flanked by UN Secretary General Ban Ki-moon, Prince Philip would accept a total of thirty-one plans. 'Many Heavens, One Earth' was a memorable occasion. With nine different religions and accompanying rituals and dietary instructions, the ARC staff had a big job on their hands, but with the UN on board, they also had to grapple with a whole host of safety regulations. Their efforts were more than rewarded. On a sunny, crystal-clear winter's afternoon in November, the starting shot sounded to mark the beginning of a rare but colourful and inspirational event. The impressive, sturdy British castle with its creamy-grey stone walls was a beautiful backdrop for all those colourful garments and banners from the various traditions. It was downright inspirational to experience the passion and devotion with which these faiths showed their commitment to making their environment more sustainable. There was an atmosphere of inspiration and fellowship at all levels. In a witty and moving speech, Prince Philip talked about the origins of ARC and how the success of the WWF 25th anniversary meeting with the religions ran away with him and Martin, the present gathering at Windsor marking the high point for the moment. Ban Ki-moon also shared his thoughts with the audience and even allowed himself to improvise some of his speech, something that hardly ever happens in the carefully orchestrated performances of UN secretary generals. He said that the religious leaders who had gathered together had more opportunity, scope and spirit than anybody else to get the world moving. In his opinion, the religions together with their own communities had the strength to stimulate political leaders to accept responsibility for transforming the future of our planet into a sustainable reality. When he finished his speech, he was given a standing ovation.

The nine religions then took turns to present their multi-year plans. And there they were: the Daoists on stage between Prince Philip and Ban Ki-moon, posing for the ubiquitous press and handing over their Eight-Year plan. Their performance took no more than three minutes but to me it was a moving sight. This was how far we had travelled with the Daoists, who in the process had become a very important part of my life. It was wonderful proof that the wisdom of Daoism was alive and well and more relevant than ever. It was great to see how the event gave every religion both space and respect as they showed their commitment, each in their own way and according to the rituals of their own tradition. I couldn't help thinking that the world would be much more peaceful if all these religions could get along equally well outside such special occasions. It was clearly possible. If the reality was very different, then it was not because of religious writings but because of the way humanity had interpreted and used these writings over the centuries. History teaches us that all too often religion has political connotations. This is certainly true for Daoism, which in the dynastic period was alternately embraced and repudiated by the imperial rulers. And even today, the Communist Party wastes no time in channelling and tapping into the smouldering spiritual awareness and desire of its subjects to suit its own agenda. This is exactly what makes ARC's position so precarious. Where do you draw the line between helping the Daoists deploy ancient traditions to create a more sustainable world, and accommodating an authoritarian system that uses religion as an instrument of control? I have often wondered about that, especially in light of the chasm in China between the organised and the organic, and the consequent, deep-rooted distrust between the Chinese state and its people. When I shared these thoughts with Martin, he said he could relate to what I was saying. He told me that ARC's main goal was to give religions worldwide enough leeway to discover or rediscover ecological principles without sacrificing their traditions and rituals. There is a link with nature in all religious traditions but, in times of global political and economic turbulence, nature gets pushed to the background. ARC helps the religions regrow their ecological roots and turn them into practical action and commitment to sustainability. Sometimes, as in China's case, that mission is much more politically charged than might seem at first glance. In China, it's simply not possible to operate outside the state's field of vision. This is certainly true for the rebuilding of a temple and a nationwide programme to broach a thorny issue like ecology, and via Daoism of all things. But these very same initiatives might also allow interests to converge. When the state acknowledged that China's environment is in trouble and religion might mobilise support for any solutions, ARC found it had a bigger margin for negotiation—and hence for Daoist religious practice. For the moment, the high point was the Dao De Jing Forum, where the whole of Daoism was celebrated as a source of wisdom, core of Chinese identity and guiding light for the problems the country was facing. It was an ironic wink to history, Martin decided, in a country where an atheist state had spent decades trying to scrap 'Daoism' from the dictionary.

In 2011, the International Daoist Forum was held near Heng Shan, the southern sacred mountain in the province of Hunan. As was the case for the Xian Forum in 2007, the event was controlled by SARA and CDA headquarters. I may have had to miss Xian but now I could see for myself how the Chinese state was shaping its newly found interest in Daoism. The conference was certainly a memorable event. The opening ceremony had an air of Olympic grandeur. A magnificent and enchanting ballet acted out texts from the Dao De Jing to the music of no less a composer than 'local' Oscar winner Tan Dun. A gigantic projection screen created a backdrop of breathtaking images matching the text and choreography. It was absolutely spectacular. No expense or effort had been spared. Apparently, much could be achieved if the state lent its support. What a contrast with the budget for the workshops in Taibai Shan and Jurong. I think it was halfway through the show that Martin whispered: "Bit of a change from karaoke and a barbeque in a square somewhere on a remote mountain slope."

No fewer than five hundred participants had registered for the forum and additional chairs had to be pulled up right from the word go. This time, participants did not only come from Daoist circles in China but also from Hong Kong, Taiwan, Macao, South Korea and Singapore. As expected, there were party officials, researchers and other specialists from Chinese and foreign universities, as well as Chinese captains of business. The interest from business in particular seemed a favourable development. On top of these groups, the Chinese media turned up en masse to cover the event. On this occasion, the question was how the wisdom of Daoism could be deployed to solve the social and ecological problems currently facing China. The theme was perfectly encapsulated by a recent event that had gripped Chinese society in the preceding weeks. The media had been full of the story of a two-year-old toddler in a Guangzhou street who had been hit by several passing cars and died of her injuries while not a single one of some twenty passers-by did anything to help. The nation was outraged and the incident was widely seen as evidence of the moral bankruptcy of Chinese society. Many conference speakers referred to the incident in their plea for a return to the Daoist principles of compassion, moderation and humility. Everyone heard Wang Zuoan, Director of SARA, argue that in the current age of globalisation, China could draw inspiration from Daoism—not only to protect nature but also to protect hearts and souls. Xu Jialu, a former vice-chairman of the National People's Congress Standing Committee, also noted that humanity needed the wisdoms of the old sages more than ever. These wisdoms are close to the essence of the world, unlike the twisted age we live in today. It was clear that all levels of the political establishment not only accepted Daoism but regarded it as a source of wisdom and inspiration for the government of the nation. Martin recalled what a truly historical moment it was. The last time the Daoists had been consulted about affairs of state by a political leader had been in 1219—by Genghis Khan of all people.

Martin was one of the keynote speakers and he again came armed with a message of congratulation from Prince Philip, which was much appreciated and extensively covered in the media. I also had the honour of giving a presentation in one of the parallel sessions that took place in the following days. I was very pleased I could elaborate on the long, long history of Daoism and ecology and give an eye witness report on the progress of the Daoist Ecology Temple Alliance so far. We were also invited for an audience with Mr Wang. I remember we were received in a spacious, richly decorated room. There was no table and the chairs were lined up at equal intervals against the walls. It reminded me of my meetings with ministers in Taiwan in the late 1970s. The informal discussion confirmed the seriousness of the government's intentions.

But the absolute high point of the event was not so much any single speech or the declaration presented at the end but a special plenary session with all the participants and guests in front of the cameras of CCTV, China's state television broadcaster. In the preparation phase, the idea had been floated to use prime-time television for a discussion about the role of Daoism in tackling the problems confronting present-day China. To this end, Xu Jialu had been invited to represent the state. Who should represent the Daoists was hotly debated between SARA and CDA. Martin told me in genuine surprise and modesty that in the end they had unanimously decided the role should be his. And that's how Martin ended up in a TV debate, before millions of Chinese viewers, to explain what gave Daoism its power and why its wisdoms could persuade and move entire nations. ARC's leading man had not only helped to get the Daoists and the state—the bottom and the top—back to the table but had himself grown to become the face of a revived Daoism.

Who would have guessed in 1989 that this might be the outcome when I saw the contemptuous looks of the Taiwanese authors of the *Taiwan 2000 Report*? Who could have predicted such an outcome when Martin and I met for the first time over dinner? Who would have dared entertain such a hope when, in 2005, we inaugurated a piece of land on a mountain where a Daoist temple should have stood? Or was it all just serendipity?

Nothing in the world

is softer than water...

—but we know it can wear away

the hardest of things.

The supple

Overcomes the hard,

And the so-called weak, the strong.

People know this, but no one quite believes it.

...And the truth is that the truth

is often a paradox.

Chapter 78 of the Dao De Jing

6

What Next?

China's Balancing Act

Heng Shan was of course a huge milestone. Never before in the previous century had a Chinese government embraced Daoism so openly. What's more, the last time a Chinese ruler had asked the Daoists for policy advice was some eight hundred years before. History was being written and it was a privilege to be part of it. But for a down-to-earth Dutchman like me, it did raise a question: what next? Would Daoism be able to expand its position and scope in Chinese society? And if so, how? And equally important: would it be in time to put a stop to the reckless exploitation of China's environment? We were on the brink of environmental catastrophe and to me it looked decidedly like Taiwan in the 1980s. It seemed as if there had been a wholesale shift of Taiwanese face masks, grey smog and discoloured rivers across the straits to mainland China.

Newspaper pictures of Beijing residents covering their mouths against what looks like a thick pinkish-grey smog make me gasp for air every time. According to figures published by the World Bank in 2007, sixteen of the twenty most polluted cities in the world are in China. Only 1 per cent of the 560 million Chinese city-dwellers breathe air that would pass standards deemed acceptable in the European Union. Some 500 million Chinese don't have access to safe drinking water. Rivers are heavily polluted as a result of illegal (and sometimes legal) toxic discharge, chemical waste buried in the ground and intensive sand and stone mining. Some rivers are even toxic themselves. Vast swathes of

Chinese coastal waters are so polluted that they no longer support marine life. The World Bank, in collaboration with the Chinese State Environmental Protection Administration (renamed Ministry of Environmental Protection in 2008), has calculated that the high pollution levels cause approximately 760,000 premature deaths in China every year. The figures were kept out of the final World Bank Report at the request of SEPA, which was concerned about social unrest. It is indicative of how the Chinese government has dealt with the environmental crisis up to this point. Reliable figures are scarce, downplayed or denied, and the resulting social unrest is bought off or suppressed. A typical example is the row between the United States Embassy in Beijing and the Beijing Municipal Environmental Protection Bureau in June 2012. The Americans sounded the alarm over excessive levels of fine dust particles in the air, while the Chinese observatory called the quality of the air satisfactory. The Chinese state then threw out the American measurements, arguing that they were 'unscientific', and requested that foreign agencies refrain from publishing figures in future. This hasn't stopped many Beijing residents from installing two apps on their smartphones—a Chinese and an American one—so they can monitor the quality of the city's air themselves.

These are alarming figures that make me shudder, just as 1980s Taiwan did. I again see before me a picture of an economic miracle about to turn into an ecological disaster. And it's not as if the state is closing its eyes to the problem, which is being acknowledged at the highest levels. With every environmental scandal, new measures are taken, sometimes as a token but often real. In this sense, winds of change are blowing through government at the highest levels. The problem resides at lower levels. Here, the wind loses its force. Agencies responsible for enforcement lack resources and room for manoeuvre. It's also an open secret that every rule or regulation can be circumvented with favours or money. And most important of all: there is a lack of political will. Government officials prefer scoring with economic growth than with ecological performance. The mantra of economic growth pervades the entire state apparatus and beats ecology at all levels. There is a glaring disequilibrium between economy and ecology. It's Taiwan all over again.

And I discovered even more parallels between the political and social landscapes of Taiwan and China. In Taiwan, the turning point in the government's attitude towards ecology came in response to loud protests from its own citizens. It wasn't so much the alarming figures *per se* or the images of deplorable living conditions that worried the government but the social discontent it created from the late 1970s onwards. At first, the authoritarian government could easily suppress the protests. But as the unrest intensified and began to impinge on the economy, the government could no longer ignore the problems. The decision in 1986 by international chemical giant DuPont to withdraw a planned investment after strong public protests had an immediate effect on the government coffers.

Having followed developments in China from the sidelines for a number of years now, I'm starting to see a similar pattern there. In the first few decades of a booming economy from the late 1970s onwards, the environmental effects were not really visible and the gain in welfare led to relative social quiet. Ironically, the very same economic progress made a growing, comfortable middle class realise that they could and should be more concerned about the deteriorating environment. The result has been a quadrupling in the last ten years of the number of public protests in the wake of environmental scandals. The environment is in fact one of the main sources of social unrest in China. The protests are mostly organised by a growing, well-educated, urban middle class but are increasingly spreading to China's rural interior. An expanding network of well-informed environmental activists, often based in the larger cities, and social media savvy, can galvanise larger and larger numbers of people throughout the whole country.

The parallels with Taiwan are clear. But I saw that these similarities actually apply universally, to any country anywhere in the world. Every country as well as every form of government intervention rests on three elements: economy, ecology (or the natural environment) and society (or the social, cultural structure of a community). These pillars display strong interdependencies. Economic growth, for instance, affects the social structure of a community and can also affect the physical territory of a country. This is clearly demonstrated by developments in China and Taiwan. Conversely, changes in the physical landscape can impact economic opportunities and societal structures. The desertification of large tracts of land in the north (and more recently in the south) of China is having an enormous impact on the opportunities for economic and social development in traditional farming communities. And as the emergence of an environmental movement in China (and similarly in Taiwan) is showing, social change can affect economic and ecological development.

Not only are the three pillars mutually dependent but my experiences with China have shown me that each of these pillars is governed by its own dynamics: an interplay between the state and the people—between the organised top and an organically grown bottom—with the balance continually shifting. Nowhere is the dynamic of that interplay so sharply delineated as in this authoritarian country with its well-developed community culture.

Whenever the balance between top and bottom changes in one of the pillars, the effect can spill over to the other pillars. The development of the well-known Three Gorges Dam in China is a striking example of a top-down economic decision with disastrous consequences for the ecological and social pillars. The initial plans for this enormous dam across the Yangtze River in the western province of Hubei go back to 1919, as a response to the many floods that threatened the downstream villages and towns every year. But it would take until 1994 before the plans for a hydroelectric power station were ready and construction could begin. Building works were completed in 2006 and the entire project was completed in 2012 when the final turbine was fully functional. At a price of 26 billion US dollars, China was now the owner of the world's largest hydropower plant. At full capacity, it could yield 84.7 GWh. of sustainably generated electricity every year, enough to meet more than a fifth of the annual consumption of electricity in the UK. The dam eased the danger of flooding along the Yangtze and also facilitated shipping between Chongqing and Shanghai. It was a groundbreaking project in every respect, but the opening celebrations in 2006 were more than overshadowed by the ecological and social problems that dogged the project. A telling detail is that then President Hu Jintao and Premier Wen Jiabao—themselves hydraulic engineers— were not present at the opening.

Critics had from the outset pointed to the danger of landslides and earthquakes resulting from pressure under the 400-mile-long basin,

pollution and salinisation of the river, and climate change caused by
a disrupted water cycle. In addition, the project displaced some 1.5
million people and simply submerged about one thousand villages as
well as numerous archaeological and cultural heritage sites. The people
most affected were farmers who had to leave their land and were given
the choice of moving to the city or accepting a piece of land higher up.
Those who chose the latter often had to cut down trees and prepare
the land before they could do any kind of farming, only to find the
land eroding from under their feet. The new city dwellers were moved
to neighbourhoods hurriedly created for the purpose, with drab
tenement blocks and far removed from their former traditional lifestyle, close to nature and the community. The net outcome was usually
abject poverty. They either lived in a city, where farming skills had
little value, or on a worthless, infertile piece of land that could barely
support anyone. And on top of all this, there was the mental blow of
yet another radical change in the lives of a generation who had already
suffered so much under Mao's sweeping overhaul.

As early as 2007, a senior party official closely involved with the
project pointed out its 'hidden dangers'. But not until 2011 did I read
in the paper that Premier Wen Jiabao had officially acknowledged
'pressing geological, ecological and humanitarian problems' with the
Three Gorges Dam. At a single stroke, China's showpiece was officially
degraded to a vanity project. To me, it was solid proof that an instrument of power should not be deployed freely from the top of the
economic pillar—sooner or later the bottom of the ecological and
social pillars will rise in revolt. So imagine my surprise when I heard
from Claudia that the Chinese government had embarked on another
large-scale project, namely the South-North Water Transfer Project, an
ambitious scheme to divert huge quantities of water from the Yangtze
to China's arid north through a system of canals and other waterways
to meet the needs of some major consumers such as mining and
agriculture. With the northern Yellow River too polluted, the oft-
plagued Yangtze has to quench their thirst. Once again, hundreds of
thousands of people are being forced to move and who knows what the
ecological consequences will be. The sad irony is that the calculations
underlying this megaproject come from figures on the water capacity
of the Yangtze in the 1990s. But southern China today is grappling with

an unprecedented drought and the overconsumption of water in
the southern provinces has reduced the water level to a worrying low.
So this project is heading for disaster.

Again, I couldn't believe my ears. Had nothing been learnt from the
recent past? It reminded me of the Russian Perebroska project in the
late 1960s, Stalin's megaplan to divert the flow of five northern rivers
southwards. At least 70,000 researchers and engineers pored over the
problem for several decades. Here too, entire villages were moved and
obliterated. Canals were built with nuclear explosives of all things,
leaving nothing but a useless, radioactive wasteland. The money-
gobbling project left a trail of ecological and social destruction before
it was abandoned in the 1980s under then President Gorbachev.

Western Europe has its own major water project failure, namely
the Spanish Ebro River plan. Here, the government launched a scheme
in 2011 to provide water from the Ebro in the north to the arid south
by means of some one hundred dams and canals running hundreds
of miles. Despite opposition from environmentalists, financial specialists and even the European Commission, the government at the time
pushed ahead with the plan for the hefty sum of 6 billion euros. Three
years later, the project was discontinued after all because of the ecological and financial risks.

So there is no shortage of disturbing examples. Nonetheless,
the Chinese government again wants to go for the economic pillar,
top-down and without due consideration of or accountability to the
ecological and social pillars. Such thoughts are not exactly encouraging
and I keep wondering when the turnaround will come and if it will
come in time to preserve China's environment from further catastrophe. I realise at the same time that any turnaround can and will
not come from the state alone. When the state apparatus is so strongly
developed and sails its own course, it behaves like a supertanker on the
high seas—it is slow and cannot change direction easily. But no matter
how well-organised or removed from society, the state cannot endlessly
ignore public sentiment at the organic level of the ecological and social
pillars. In each of the three pillars, the state and its people are bound
together in a complex give-and-take.

What has become very clear to me in the last few years is that religion
can play an important role. This is especially true in a country like

China, where the state and society have developed their own dynamic and are so diametrically opposed and where religious traditions are very tied up with the culture, social structure and identity of the people. On my adventures in China, I've been able to see and experience how ARC has used and shaped the role of religion in an effective and respectful way. Through marginal action, Martin and his team have managed to build a bridge between the state and society. By beating their drum at the right moment and in the right tone, ARC has helped to ensure that ecology and religion—two politically sticky issues—are on the current agenda of the Chinese state. With the construction of the Taibai Shan Daoist Ecology Temple and the workshops, ARC and the Daoists have managed to disseminate the message of ecological awareness amongst the Chinese Daoist community in a very practical, timely and pervasive fashion. The resulting national and international attention has helped persuade the state to embrace Daoism as a potential way of solving the current ecological and social problems afflicting the country. Since the first International Daoist Forum in 2007, the state has officially declared that the wisdom of Daoist tradition must return to the heart of society in order to stem corruption, moral decay and unbridled materialism. In the fight against these plagues, the Daoist notions of compassion, moderation and humility are a welcome antidote and will help restore a 'harmonious society'. In October 2013, I heard the highest official at the Chinese Embassy in the UK underline this sentiment during the opening of a CDA exhibition on Daoism in London. It remains to be seen how effectively the state can propagate such a new social morality without taking a good look in the mirror. But what cannot be denied is that it has given the Daoists credit for their traditions and scope for development.

As far as the ecological pillar goes, hope might spring from the resolution issued by the Third Plenum of the current government, the party meeting where economic policy and future reform are planned. The word 'ecology' is mentioned more often than ever before and, for the first time ever, ecology and society each take up just as much space as the economy. The wording in such statements is traditionally broad and vague and only time will tell whether party officials down the line feel it incumbent upon themselves to implement the new policies and reforms. It would already make a difference if current environmental

policy were actually enforced. At present, many regulations fall victim to bribery and the personal whim of local officials. But it is certainly encouraging to read that current President Xi Jinping and Premier Li Keqiang, who took office in March 2013, have committed themselves to the anti-corruption policy of their predecessors. Even more encouraging is that, more than ever before, citizens are finding their way to the courts to secure compliance with the law. Environmental activists have already filed the first lawsuits against polluting companies. I expect that this movement towards ecological awareness will gather pace and spread from the bottom upwards. And I remain absolutely convinced of my conclusions in *The Transformation Factor*. The movement will fan out from the level of communities that are rooted in age-old traditions but have evolved into a kind of modern citizenry and identity. Developments like the internet and social media are producing a well-informed, creative and vocal populace despite attempts by the authorities to silence protests. The confrontation between rulers and ruled is increasingly shifting to the internet, to a more transparent and open digital world. Social media is making it harder for the state to ignore or suppress the protests. In February 2013, for example, a Chinese journalist called on people to share photos of polluted rivers in their own neighbourhood via Weibo, the Chinese hybrid equivalent of Twitter and Facebook. This was how he raised local environmental scandals to the national stage. The state has been presented with a healthy management dilemma: local is no longer local.

The modern form of citizenship goes hand in hand with a renewed interest in old tradition and religion. The growth in welfare produced by the booming Chinese economy since the 1980s has also generated meaningful questions about identity and religious awareness among the rapidly expanding middle class. And it doesn't end there. Religion has given hope and support to rural communities that have been uprooted and relocated to anonymous city neighbourhoods as part of large-scale urbanisation and other projects. There are no reliable figures on the number of religious Chinese but estimates suggest that about one third of the population openly profess a religious affiliation. The number is still growing, with Buddhism far in the lead. Interest in Daoism is also rising steadily, especially among the younger generation of Chinese born after the Cultural Revolution. They are looking for the roots of their cultural background and identity. I remember the moderator of the televised debate Martin took part in during the International Daoist Forum in Heng Shan. Just before the cameras began to roll, she spoke a few words to the audience. Her gaze travelled past the endless rows of monks and nuns in their blackish-blue robes and she said she was genuinely surprised there were so many practising Daoist masters. She had never realised this and felt truly inspired. To me, it was wonderful that this very intelligent, modern, young Chinese woman seemed so moved by her discovery that Daoism, a tradition she probably never encountered in daily life, appeared very much alive and part of her own background.

A telling fact for the advance of religion in China is the growing body of opinion favouring the restoration within Confucianism of its religious liturgical tradition. At an ARC conference in 2013, I met Professor Tu Weiming, world-renowned authority on Neo-Confucianism. He felt that the state had made a major mistake when it purged all spiritual elements from the state philosophy of Confucianism. Rules imposed from above should not be followed blindly; they should be anchored in something that has personal meaning and morality. He saw it as his mission to bring spirituality back to this most Chinese of traditions. It's a view that meshes perfectly with ARC's mission. And so it happened that, in the summer of 2013, ARC could welcome the Confucianists as the twelfth cultural tradition. With the foundation of the International Confucian Ecological Alliance (ICEA) and the ecological statement with which they joined ARC, the Confucianists committed themselves for the first time in history to nature conservation and other ecological goals. Martin and I were invited to ICEA's inaugural meeting and each gave a speech. Following their successful work with the Daoists, ARC also assisted ICEA with concrete projects in the area of environmental education programmes, greener cultural practices and the development of a multi-year plan. The subject of ecology, for instance, will become part of the permanent curriculum of Confucian educational institutions. In this way, the message imparted by ecology can be made to echo throughout China's state machinery.

Apart from the Confucianists, ARC has also spent the last few years reaching out to the Chinese Buddhists, the largest religious group in China. In 2010, Martin and I were invited by Abbot Jue Xing of the magnificent Jade Buddha Monastery in Shanghai to a seminar, where the Buddhists had a close look at their role in nature conservation. Martin and I gave presentations so we could share the experiences we'd had with the Daoists and the results achieved. What I remember most is that we landed in a completely different atmosphere from the meetings with the Daoists. Whereas the Daoist workshops had been downright austere, the Buddhists had put us up in the most luxurious hotel rooms, treated us to exquisite meals, and held meetings in state-of-the-art conference rooms, all on the premises of the monastery. To me, it seemed a peculiar manifestation of the fact that historically Daoism is the religion of the rural poor, while Buddhism appeals to affluent urbanites. Or as Martin once explained: on a Daoist sacred mountain, you are part of a robust natural environment that makes you feel humble and inspires unity with your surroundings; whereas on a Buddhist sacred mountain, you're just a human observer and a visitor.

But above all, ARC and I will of course continue our relationship with the Daoists, at grass-roots level via the Daoist Ecology Temple Alliance, Master Ren and Professor Fan, as well as at state level via SARA and CDA. The Temple Alliance's third Ecology Workshop has already been slated for April 2014. The sessions will focus on expanding the network and launching new, nationwide campaigns. In addition, there are advanced plans for other projects whose aim is to spread the message of sustainability in practical ways and reinforce the position of the Daoists in the international network of ARC.

These projects will help raise ecological awareness at the level of society. But more is required if the megaprojects brewed up by the state, like the South-North Water project, are to be halted. The state will have to take more account of the ecological and social pillars and build bridges with provincial and local levels. And it can be done. It can even be done quickly. If semi-capitalist, authoritarian China has shown us anything at all, it's that it can make huge investments to realise megaprojects in no time. I discovered this myself on my travels with Martin. Nowadays, we no longer need to fly across China to cover the huge distances. We travel by ultramodern, comfortable high-speed trains. And so do many Chinese because the trains were jam-packed. In precisely the eight years I have regularly travelled through China with ARC, the state has invested as much as 5 billion US dollars to get a high-speed rail network up and running. Travelling at an average speed of almost 200 miles per hour, with excellent service from neatly dressed hostesses, travel information in Chinese and English, and a punctuality many railways elsewhere in the world could only dream of, Martin and I raced through the country in October 2013 on our way to the Daoists and Confucianists. A striking detail at the futuristic stations where we stopped, and where our every need was met, was that there was always a corner set aside for a tea room offering travellers tea prepared in the traditional way. Young Chinese waiters took their time to prepare the tea in a lengthy ceremony. There was no rush, no gimmickry, just a patient steeping of tea leaves in not-quite-boiling water until fully brewed. It was great to see innovation and tradition share the same platform and to feel time stand still for just a moment amid the rushing trains. Such an ultramodern rail network shows that China is capable of acting quickly and successfully. The authoritarian government is indeed able to realise big projects and apply the latest technologies swiftly and effectively. And this gives hope. At the same time, recent history teaches us that hope can turn into catastrophe when the social and ecological consequences of major investments are ignored. The South-North Water project threatens to be yet another example.

But there is an alternative, namely a model where economic growth goes hand in hand with the development of sustainable value chains in production and agriculture, based on the principle of Reduce, Reuse and Recycle. This is the 'circular economy', the counterpart of the 'linear economy', where products made from finite natural resources ultimately end up on the rubbish dump. The model stems from the 1970s and has been on the rise at European Union level for a number of years now. And here's the good news: as early as 2006, China launched the circular economy in its Eleventh Five-Year Plan as a spearhead of national policy. The highest levels of government are fully aware that the focus on economic growth brings with it an unprecedented demand for energy and fresh water. These are the basic ingredients of economic growth and such levels of demand cannot be satisfied in the conventional, linear, economic manner. In its circular economy programme, the central government has set the scene for economic development based on sustainable energy, efficient use of natural resources, clean production, eco-design and sustainable consumption. And given

China's current water problems, the contributing role of agriculture and the South-North Water plans, we should add to the list a sustainable water supply and sustainable agriculture. In the last few years, various cities, industrial zones and branches of industry have been part of pilots for the Chinese circular economy programme, some with participation from the United Nations Environmental Programme and the European Commission. The current government too has boosted budgets for the promotion of the circular economy.

So there seems to be commitment at the top. Moreover, as long as there is support rather than corruption or intransigence at lower levels of government, the central government should also have the ability to achieve a circular economy. The country has shown it can deploy large-scale, state-of-the-art technology. Now, if it were to adopt decentralised, smaller-scale solutions, then a sustainable supply of water and energy might indeed become a reality.

Circular economy is pre-eminently a model that thrives on a local, decentralised approach and the development of local solutions. It offers great opportunities for solving China's water shortages, in particular. We only have to look at the Spanish Ebro project. The Spanish government responded to the cancellation of that costly project by selecting the much cheaper solution of local and regional desalination plants to address the fresh water shortage. China could deploy the many smaller-scale technologies for sustainable freshwater systems as an alternative to the South-North Water project. The last few years have seen very rapid technological progress in this area. The most recent innovations have withstood the scepticism that often prevails vis-à-vis small-scale water solutions. Nowadays, many such solutions are economically viable and ecologically justifiable. And if China were to tap into its unparalleled capacity to roll out such small-scale solutions in Chinese large-scale fashion, it might have a sustainable way of meeting its huge demand for water. At the very least, it might stem a continuous decline in the water table, which in the area of Beijing has dropped by more than 65 feet since 1970. And this is no exception: in the last few decades, the arid north of China has seen the water table drop by as much as 4 feet every year. With expanding metropoles like Beijing, coal mining in the far north and agricultural activity, China's thirst keeps growing. The economic, ecological and social consequences of the water shortage hang above the country like the sword of Damocles.

Small-scale, regional solutions for sustainable water and energy provision, clean production chains and recycling can provide China with a concrete solution to the problems it's currently facing. If the central government embraces initiatives emanating from the population, the growing middle class and the new entrepreneurs, the result will be a sustainable basis for a successful Chinese circular economy.

And this is where Daoism can play a role. The wisdoms of Daoism and principles of circular economy correspond very nicely: Daoism sees the laws of nature reflected in the human body and even society and, similarly, the ideas behind circular economy draw on living systems in nature. Furthermore, Daoism is a perfect example of a tradition entrenched at the local level and, for many Chinese, it resides just below the surface under a thin layer of atheism. And Daoism has a further side that Martin pointed out to me once. It is a tradition that challenges authority in a fundamental way. It expects individuals to return to their own inner wisdom and views every form of coerced morality as a lack of connection with the Dao. In past times, it made Daoism vulnerable and the prime target of attack from the most totalitarian regime in China's history. But in the present age of change, of greater economic freedom, of social problems that seem to be eating away at the roots of the political system and of internet and social media, Daoism might offer the nation the inspiration needed to find a sustainable solution.

If Daoism can inspire the growing entrepreneurial and middle classes and those looking for a healthier environment, then there is hope. And if the state has the courage to invest in local sustainability initiatives, then that hope might well be realised. The coming decades would require that government organisations integrate with organic society, including the Daoists who are an integral part of it. If this were to happen, then China could become an international standard-bearer of a sustainable society where economic, ecological, social and spiritual forces are bundled together.

If only all of these hopes are realised in time to effect the big turn-around. It's a problem facing not just China but the whole world. Do we go full steam ahead or do we stop and think? Do we reflect on where we're heading? In China, the time is ripe for a closer contemplation of things and Daoism has much to offer here. This is especially true in an age where the country is grappling with a multitude of conflicting forces: communism versus capitalism, atheism versus religion, centralisation versus decentralisation, large-scale versus small-scale, opaqueness versus transparency, and an organised versus an organic society. These pairs are opposites and inextricably linked at the same time. Whether China can achieve some kind of equilibrium will hinge on its ability to find proper trade-offs. This will require a delicate balancing act—one that will determine the future both within and beyond China's borders. It surely can't be coincidence that the Daoist yin-yang symbol expresses just such a balancing act...

How this will materialise, I can't say. Going with the flow, not going against the grain, sensing the right time, not acting if there's no need: these are all maxims of the Daoist principle of *wu-wei*. At least, this is how I have come to understand the principle on my journey through Daoism. To me, marginal action is the practical translation of *wu-wei* and I have had the pleasure of discovering the value of this strategy with ARC.

And so I continue my journey, up the sacred mountain. At certain moments, I take the time to absorb the views from the mountain. I look. I listen. And I hear the sounds of the world.

Pictures

Guan Yin

Top: Iron tree

Middle: Speeching

Bottom: Workshop 2005

Top: Taibai Shan inauguration ceremony

Middle: Incense burner

Bottom: Martin, Allerd

Top: Mountain brook

Middle: Xiaoxin, Allerd, Master Ren, Martin, Professor Fan, Peter

Bottom: Temple inauguration 2007

Top: Mao Shan temples

Bottom: Mao Shan workshop 2008

Top: President China Daoist Association, Master Ren, UNDP Deputy Director, Olav Kjørven

Top: Lao Zi statue, Mao Shan

Top: Friends

中 央 领 导 接 见 国 际 道

Top: At Windsor castle   Bottom: Speeching

Middle: International Daoist Forum 2011

Bottom: Intermission

教 论 坛 部 分 代 表 合 影

Top: Presenting the Daoist Eight-Year Plan

Top: Daoist performance

Bottom: Xu Jialu and Martin in TV debate

Bottom: Symbolic handing out of *Lao Zi Commentaries* by Minister Wang

Appendices

Qinling Declaration (2006)

Harmony between Heaven, Earth and Humanity is the crucial guarantee for the sustainability of human activities on earth. It is the highest aim of Daoists. With the environmental crisis getting worse day by day, we have a duty to rethink the role of Daoism in China, and to consider how we can make a better contribution to the environment today. All the attendants of the first workshop on Daoism and Conservation have reached an agreement to set up a **Daoist Temple Alliance on Ecology Education**. In order to build up ecologically-friendly Daoist temples, we promise to introduce the following six key action points to the construction processes, management and religious practices of all our temples.

The Key Action Points are:
1. To introduce ecological education into our temple programmes, particularly in the context of temple construction.
2. To reduce the pollution caused by incense burners and related fireworks.
3. To use our farmed land in a sustainable way.
4. To pay close attention to the protection of local species and to sustainable forestry.
5. To use energy-saving technology.
6. To protect nearby water resources.

We will inform each other of our progress in implementing these action points, and will share our experiences and the lessons we have learned, in order to welcome the 2007 workshop on Daoism and Conservation through real achievements and actions.

The Mao Shan Declaration (2008)

In 2008, an earthquake hit Wen Chuan in Sichuan Province and the Olympics were held in Beijing. In this bittersweet autumn, sixty-nine representatives from Chinese Daoist temples and associations have gathered together in Mao Shan—a blissful place in Southeast China—to discuss ways to counter the global ecological crisis with international environmental organizations in order to build a better homeland.

The Daoist philosophy and Daoist religion both emphasize the values of life and nature. They see everything as equal, and the world as a whole, so that when one thing gets hurt, others will be harmed, and when one thing is protected, others will share the benefit. In today's world, climate change, natural disasters and environment pollution have become our real concerns. But we are also in a good era, a time when the whole country is united, science has been greatly developed and harmony has become a shared goal. The Daoist faiths therefore recognize that it is necessary to inherit our old tradition, while also advancing with time, and to innovate and make progress.

The Ecology Protection Forum of China Daoist Temples and Pagodas follows the principle that the 'Dao Follows Nature' and sees the pursuit of harmony between heaven and human as its obligation. It calls for all Daoists to change our feelings and behavior to realize the sacred goal that we share: to build ecological temples and forge our heaven on earth.

Based on Daoist principles, we hold Lao Zi as our God of Ecology. We advocate a better use of land, forest and water resources, and we call for all the faithful to make the landscape in and around Daoist temples greener and more beautiful. We will also put in place proper facilities that will help protect our water resources and deal with pollution, build systematic plans and regulations that will help to promote environment protection programs, and education, and use energy saving technology and materials in order to build a benign ecological link between living areas and the natural environment.

We also promise that in the next ten years, our ecological temples project will focus on the following seven areas:
1. Putting great effort into ecological education and training. Expanding materials and education about the natural environment, that will be open to pilgrims and ordinary people who visit our temples and mountains.
2. Advocating simpler lifestyles that will reduce energy and energy costs.
3. Participating in Social environmental activities with the community.
4. To enhance cooperation with the media to spread the word about ecology.
5. To build ecological temples as our duty.
6. Maximizing the ecological benefit we can achieve from our assets.
7. Building and maintaining a Daoist Ecological Protection Network.

Eight-Year Plan for Ecological Protection (2009)

Summary 2010–2017

Education
- Daoist temples will hold regular Daoist ecological protection forums, share teachings on the environment, set up information boards on ecological issues in prominent places as well as create and explain environmental construction standards. The target is that, by 2015, half of all Daoist temples in mainland China will have educational projects under way.
- The temples will gradually set up volunteer teams who will work together with relevant communities and thus spread Daoist ecological thinking to the wider society.
- The Daoists will run regular youth camps for young people from urban China and overseas to spend time in nature, stay healthy as a result and learn about protecting the environment.
- The China Daoist Association will help Daoist temples form an alliance of ecology temples and healthcare temples to promote the connection between an ecologically friendly lifestyle and a healthy one.

Resources
Daoists will:
- Restore buildings and facilities on Daoist-used land and erect new temples according to traditional wisdom. From 2010 to 2012, they will draw up an ecological action plan and, from 2013 to 2017, they will promote their experiences of ritual, education, recycling, living, the media, etc. to temples across the country.
- Protect the water resources around temples and deal effectively with sewage.

- Plant trees and other vegetation around the temples, with specific attention to protecting old trees, and create natural meditation and walking areas. They have already opened up such areas in and around a few temples. From 2012 onwards, they will promote this practice in the grounds of suitable Daoist temples across the country.
- Call for a healthier and more environmentally friendly style of pilgrimage and travel. The main target will be the 'three-stick-incense-burning' policy, whereby temples promote the burning of just three incense sticks instead of the current many sticks. This will reduce air pollution and provide a positive signal for China's wealthy to adopt a simpler and more modest life. Daoists also recommend offerings of flowers and fruit as an alternative to burning incense.
- Use only environmentally friendly religious articles.
- Prohibit the use of ingredients derived from endangered animals and plants in all Daoist healthcare food and medicinal remedies.
- Make sure that temples with restaurants and lodging manage these places in ways that are kind to the environment, such as reducing the use of water, energy and disposable items.
- Set up Daoist medical clinics and welfare accommodation for the elderly and run these in environmentally friendly ways.

Ecological wisdom
Daoists will:
- Continue the tradition of simple and energy-saving lifestyles and promote this to visitors and pilgrims.
- Integrate ecological concepts into rituals. They have already experimented with this in some Daoist temples—for instance, writing prayers about the environment.
- Actively cooperate with forest and tourist organisations to hold activities that will help protect the Daoist sacred mountains.
- Collect traditional stories on environmental protection to provide useful lessons for today's environmental reality. From 2010 to 2013, they will collect the stories from local temples, to be published and distributed after 2014.
- Select their daily timetable and food according to natural principles.

Ecological Partnerships and Celebrations

Daoists will:

- Work within government standards, rules and regulations as well as enhance connections with international environmental organisations.
- Emphasise ecological concepts inherent to traditional Daoist festivals, such as the birthday of the Supreme Lord Lao Zi. Some provinces have already begun to preach Daoist ecological concepts during Daoist festivals. From 2010 onwards, all temples should emphasise ecological protection during both Daoist festivals and temple fairs.
- Produce Daoist ecology songs, dances and paintings, and share these art forms through TV and radio, the internet, concert celebrations and temple fairs.
- Incorporate International Environment Day activities within the Daoist religious calendar.

The Nature of the Dao and Sustainable Development: Observations by a Visitor from Europe

International Daoism Forum
Hengyang City, Hunan Province, 21-23 October 2011

As a visitor from Europe and a friend of the Dao, I feel very honoured to have been offered the opportunity to formulate some observations on the subject of sustainability and its relationship with Daoism. I am a great admirer and long-time student of Daoism, but I realise that I cannot claim any of the deep expertise and practice accumulated by the masters, scholars and other experts present at the International Daoism Forum. Nevertheless, I will take this opportunity to give you some of my views.

My experience with sustainability and Daoism goes back to the early 1980s, when I frequently visited the island of Taiwan. Though at that time Taiwan was considered the 'economic miracle of the Far East', I was struck by the effects of decades of spectacular economic growth combined with a total neglect of the ecological factor. The air, the rivers and the soil were so polluted that you could smell and see the effects everywhere, whilst the record number of people suffering from hepatitis and the damage done to biodiversity were alarming.

At the same time, as I visited many of the intact Temples on the island, I became aware of the culture of Daoism and started to read texts by Lao Zi and Zhuang Zi, both of whom emphasised the harmony between Heaven, Nature and Man or Heaven, Earth and Humanity.

These two contrasting encounters with the Chinese world were puzzling to me and I started studying in more detail what Daoism teaches us about the conservation of nature and what sustainability teaches us about that same subject. As a result, I was involved in a 3-year environmental study in Taiwan, which ultimately led to the publication of a report in 1989 called *Taiwan 2000: Matching Economic Growth with Environmental Protection*. Daoism was, however, not a major factor for the Chinese professionals participating in the study. I had to wait for 25 years to see that happen in China today. In the meantime, the United Nations report by the World Commission on Environment and Development—called *Our Common Future*—had been published in 1987. The People's Republic of China was represented on the Commission by Ma Shijun. It was in this report that the concept of sustainability was defined for the first time. I quote from the report:

Sustainable development is development that meets the needs of the present without compromising the ability of future generations to meet their own needs.

Thus the goals of economic and social development must be defined in terms of sustainability in all countries—developed or developing, market-oriented or centrally planned. Interpretations will vary, but must share certain general features and must flow from a consensus on the basic concept of sustainable development and on a broad strategic framework for achieving it.

Settled agriculture, the diversion of watercourses, the extraction of minerals, the emission of heat and noxious gases into the atmosphere, commercial forests, and genetic manipulation are all examples of human intervention in natural systems during the course of development. Until recently, such interventions were small in scale and their impact limited. Today's interventions are more drastic in scale and impact, more threatening to life-support systems and both locally and globally. This need not happen. At a minimum, sustainable development must not endanger the natural systems that support life on Earth; the atmosphere, the waters, the soils, and the living beings.

In her foreword, the Chairman of the Commission, Gro Harlem Brundtland, made the following statement:

'A global agenda for change'—this was what the World Commission on Environment and Development was asked to formulate. It was an urgent call

by the General Assembly of the United Nations:

· to propose long-term environmental strategies for achieving sustainable development by the year 2000 and beyond;
· to recommend ways concern for the environment may be translated into greater cooperation among developing countries and between countries at different stages of economic and social development and lead to the achievement of common and mutually supportive objectives that take account of the interrelationships between people, resources, environment, and development;
· to consider ways and means by which the international community can deal more effectively with environmental concerns; and
· to help to define shared perceptions of long-term environmental issues and the appropriate efforts needed to deal successfully with the problems of protecting and enhancing the environment, a long-term agenda for action during the coming decades, and aspirational goals for the world community.

The Commission has taken guidance from people in all walks of life. It is to these people—to all the peoples of the world—that the Commission now addresses itself. In so doing we speak to people directly as well as to institutions that they have established.

But first and foremost our message is directed towards people, whose well-being is the ultimate goal of all environment and development policies. In particular, the Commission is addressing the young. The world's teachers will have a crucial role to play in bringing this report to them.

If we do not succeed in putting our message of urgency through to today's parents and decision makers, we risk undermining our children's fundamental right to a healthy, life-enhancing environment.

Unless we are able to translate our words into a language that can reach the minds and the hearts of people young and old, we shall not be able to undertake the extensive social changes needed to correct the course of development.

To this end, we appeal to citizens' groups, to non-governmental organizations, to educational institutions, and to the scientific community. They have all played indispensable roles in the creation of public awareness and political change in the past. They will play a crucial part in putting the world onto sustainable development paths, in laying the groundwork for Our Common Future.

The objective of sustainable development and the integrated nature of the global environment/development challenges pose problems for institutions,

national and international, that were established on the basis of narrow
preoccupations and compartmentalized concerns.

Governments' general response to the speed and scale of global changes has
been a reluctance to recognize sufficiently the need to change themselves. The
challenges are both interdependent and integrated, requiring comprehensive
approaches and popular participation. Yet most of the institutions facing those
challenges tend to be independent, fragmented, working to relatively narrow
mandates with closed decision processes. Those responsible for managing
natural resources and protecting the environment are institutionally separated
from those responsible for managing the economy. The real world of interlocked
economy and ecological systems will not change; the policies and institutions
concerned must.

Although this was written nearly 25 years ago, I am afraid it still holds
today and, if I look at the present situation in the world of environment
and development, we still have a long way to go to achieve a true level
of sustainability. Our progress is slow and it is overdue.

Interestingly, of all the numerous institutions that were consulted
and listed on twenty pages in the report, about one thousand in all,
only four were affiliated with a religion, namely the All Africa Council
of Churches, one British Christian group and two Norwegian Christian
institutions.

In his preface to the Series on Religions of the World and Ecology,
Lawrence E. Sullivan observes:

Still, as the power to modify the world is both frightening and fascinating,
this has been subjected to reflection, particularly religious reflection, from time
immemorial to the present day. Today we have come to realize that we will
understand ecology better when we understand the religions that form the
rich soil of memory and practice, belief and relationships where life on earth is
rooted. Knowledge of these views can help us reappraise our ways and reorient
ourselves toward the sources and resources of life.

In the struggle to sustain the earth's environment as viable for future
generations, environmental studies have thus far left the role of religion
unprobed. This contrasts starkly with the emphasis given, for example, the role
of science and technology in threatening or sustaining the ecology. Ignorance
of religion prevents environmental studies from achieving its [sic] goals, for

though science and technology share many important features of human culture with religion, they leave unexplored essential wellsprings of human motivation and concern that shape the world as we know it. No understanding of the environment is adequate without a grasp of the religious life that constitutes the human societies which saturate the natural environment.

It is in line with this realisation that the idea of an Alliance of Religions and Conservation was created in Assisi in 1986 by his Royal Highness Prince Philip, who was then the International President of what is now the World Wide Fund for Nature (WWF). This was just one year before the publication of *Our Common Future* in 1987.

It is a commendable achievement of Martin Palmer, the Secretary General of ARC, that the ARC network now has affiliations with 11 faith institutions, of which the China Daoist Association, headquartered in the White Cloud Temple in Beijing, has been a very active partner since 1995, when it created the Declaration on the Environment.

With respect to Daoism and the environment, a collection of articles entitled *Daoism and Ecology* was published by Harvard University Press in 2001. One of the co-editors was Liu Xiaogan and contributors include Chinese scholars such as Chi-tim Lai, Li Yuanguo and Zhang Jiyu.

To an observer, this collection offers a wealth of insights into the relationship between Daoism and ecology. I quote a statement from the introduction:

Daoism proposes a comprehensive and radical restructuring of the way in which we conceive of our relationship to nature and our cosmic environment. This imaginative act does not readily lend itself to the solution of the prob-lems of modern society except inasmuch as it challenges the very foundations of our economic, political, scientific, and intellectual structures. At the same time, however, as Daoism becomes more influential in the West, even as it is misunderstood, it surely exerts a positive influence with respect to under-standing what it means to be embedded in a cosmic landscape. In such an understanding, 'nature' is not something outside of us to be dealt with after the fashion of a mechanic repairing a car, but is both a mental attitude to be carefully cultivated and the true condition of one's body, which contains the infinite dimensions of cosmic reality within itself. Ultimately, nature is to be constructed and visualized time and again. The terrain of our most authentic ecological concern, therefore, is first and foremost the landscape of the religious imagination.

Another contributor to *Daoism and Ecology* is Kristofer Schipper (Professor Shi Zhouren), a master of the Zhengyi school of Daoism, who spent 25 years putting together the complete canon of Daoism from 1,500 works dating back to the Ming Dynasty. On the origin of the awareness of and guidelines for the preservation of the natural environment, I quote from his article:

As early as during the first centuries of the common era, Daoism developed institutions and regulations (the 'One Hundred and Eighty Precepts'; see below) with the purpose of protecting the environment and to ensure that its natural balance would not be destroyed. It purposely advocated respect for women and children, for all forms of animal life, for all plants, for the earth, for mountains, rivers, forests and sought to preserve and protect them. These rules and institutions may be the earliest significant and conscious efforts of human civilization to protect the natural environment and to ensure the adaption [sic] of culture to nature instead of the opposite.

And on the 'One Hundred and Eighty Precepts', he writes:

One of the most important documents concerning Daoist ecology is a short text called the 'One Hundred and Eighty Precepts' (Yibaibashijie). These are guidelines laid down for those who, in the early Daoist movements, held the position of the leaders of the lay communities.

There is ample evidence, as several recent studies have shown, that 'One Hundred and Eighty Precepts' antedate the great scriptural renewal of the end of the fourth century.

Among the 'One Hundred and Eighty Precepts', not less than twenty are directly concerned with the preservation of the natural environment, and many others indirectly. Here are some examples:

14. *You should not burn (the vegetation of) uncultivated or cultivated fields, nor of mountains and forests.*
18. *You should not wantonly fell trees.*
19. *You should not wantonly pick herbs or flowers.*

36. You should not throw poisonous substances into lakes, rivers, and seas.
47. You should not wantonly dig holes in the ground and thereby destroy the earth.
53. You should not dry up wet marshes.
79. You should not fish or hunt and thereby harm and kill living beings.
95. You should not in winter dig up hibernating animals and insects.
97. You should not wantonly climb in trees to look for nests and destroy eggs.
98. You should not use cages to trap birds and (other) animals.
100. You should not throw dirty things in wells.
101. You should not seal off pools and wells.
109. You should not light fires in the plains.
116. You should not defecate or urinate on living plants or in water that people will drink.
121. You should not wantonly or lightly take baths in rivers or seas.
125. You should not fabricate poisons and keep them in vessels.
132. You should not disturb birds and (other) animals.
134. You should not wantonly make lakes.

The 'One Hundred and Eighty Precepts' cover a very wide range of topics. The text does not, however, attempt any form of organizing them according to subject, or degree of importance, or any other principle.

The emphasis on the self, on the personal relationship to the Dao, implies, also with respect to the preservation of the natural environment, that each person is responsible for the Dao, each person embodies the Dao. The preservation of the natural order therefore depends absolutely on the preservation of this natural order and harmony within ourselves and not on some outside authority. The environment is within us.

This priority of the inner world is one of the great tenets of Daoism. The outside crises and dangers can only be overcome by transforming them within us, by purifying and reshaping them through the harmony of our body. All beings are transformed through it. When it has reached perfection, the body radiates harmony that is beneficial to its environment. Thus, the 'One Hundred and Eighty Precepts' never speak of protests to higher authorities, of political actions, revindications, demands for justice and peace, but only of respiration exercises, of inner harmony and individual peace. This is the only way to save the environment. True perfect nature can only be found within oneself. To regulate the world, we have to cultivate ourselves, to tend *our inner landscape. Beyond, beneath, behind, and inside the 'Precepts' of the Daoist libationer, we find a whole new world of spiritual ecology.*

For me, as a Westerner, these texts are extremely revealing and offer me a glimpse of what Daoism is about.

The record of achievement of the China Daoist Association in revitalising the traditional respect for nature in China through a number of fora, actions and commitments in recent years is tremendously impressive and can be summarised in the following milestones:

- In 2006, the first and new Tiejiashu Daoist Ecology Temple at the foot of Taibai Mountain was ritually inaugurated. Subsequently, during a workshop with monks and nuns from ten temples in Shaanxi and Gansu provinces in Central China, the Qinling Declaration was signed with a commitment to protect the environment around their sacred lands and buildings. It was also agreed to set up a Daoist Temple Alliance on Ecology Education, with each temple to have an educational facility for that purpose. The Taibai Shan Temple was the first to have such a newly constructed facility on the premises.
- In 2008, sixty-nine representatives from Chinese Daoist temples, pagodas and associations gathered together in Mao Shan, a blissful place in southern China, to discuss with international environmental organisations various ways to counter the global ecological crisis in order to build a better homeland. This impressive gathering agreed and signed the Mao Shan Declaration, a ten-year specific commitment in six major areas, thus taking the Qinling Declaration one big step forward.
- In 2009, the China Daoist Association presented the China Daoist Ecology Protection Eight-Year Plan at a major gathering at Windsor Castle in the presence of His Royal Highness Prince Philip and UN Secretary General Ban Ki-moon and most of the faith institutes affiliated with ARC. All presented extensive seven-year plans on how they would contribute to the conservation of nature. This memorable occasion was a major milestone in reaching national consensus for the 1,500 Daoist temples in China on how to proceed for the next eight years, ending in 2017, towards fulfilling the commitments detailed in the plan.

In concluding this paper, I would like to express my gratitude and friendship to Master Ren of Lounguan Tai, who pioneered with great passion and perseverance the first Tiejiashu Daoist Ecology Temple project and who made it possible for me, a friend of the Dao, to participate right from the beginning in making his dream come true, a dream which culminated in the 2009 milestone. I am proud to have been part of the process throughout the whole period since 2005, when we first met.

None of this would have happened for me if Martin Palmer had not invited me in 2003 to join ARC in their global effort to engage the major faith institutes in the world and encourage their commitment to the conservation of nature. We both shared and continue to share a long-term connectedness with the nature of the Dao.

Allerd Stikker
Ecological Management Foundation

Acknowledgments

I am most grateful for the dedication and friendship of Maja Nijessen, Ivette Jans and Rosa Vitalie, the team who created this book with me. I am equally grateful to Martin Palmer, Master Ren Xingzhi, Professor Fan Guangchun, He Xiaoxin and He Yun (Claudia) for allowing me to join them in their heroic effort to revive Daoism in China. And, more generally, I feel immensely privileged to have been part of an incredible adventure which has enriched my world view and my life, not in the last place because of the spiritual guidance given to me by Guan Shi Yin, the Chinese Goddess of Compassion.

References

All Dao De Jing quotes are taken and, where necessary, adapted from *Tao Te Ching: The New Translation* by Man-Ho Kwok, Martin Palmer and Jay Ramsay. Element Books 1994.

The Zhuang Zi quote comes from *The Book of Chuang Tzu*, translated by Martin Palmer. Penguin Classics 2006.

The Shang Shu quote comes from *The Most Venerable Book: The Shang Shu*, translated by Martin Palmer. Penguin Classics 2014.

Also by Allerd Stikker

The Transformation Factor: Towards an Ecological Consciousness.
This work draws on both Chinese spirituality and the work of Teilhard de Chardin
as the basis for a new world view which integrates science, world religions and
interdisciplinary views of reality. Already a bestselling book in Europe, it offers a
vision of a new and harmonious relationship with nature, and is a new and valuable
guide for the ecology movement. Stikker bridges the gap between religion, philosophy and science. He relates this new synthesis to the latest trends in Western thinking
and translates this into practical conclusions and actions for today's world. This book
leads us to new understandings of human values and morality and their possible
application to science, engineering, politics, economics, art and architecture. One
of the practical outcomes for Stikker himself is the *Taiwan 2000 Report*. Here, he
explores the effect of Taiwan's economic policies on the quality of life and the
natural environment in that country.
Rockport MA, London, Brisbane: Element Books, 1992

Closing the Gap: Exploring the History of Gender Relations.
Today's patriarchal societies have their roots in antiquity, a time when matrilineal
societies gradually gave way to ancient civilisations in which men were granted more
and more importance and power—and women were made not only subordinate,
but also gradually separated from realms of the 'male'. In *Closing the Gap*, Allerd
Stikker argues that the duality between male and female is accompanied by other
dualities such as 'nature versus culture' and 'ecology versus economy'—and that
only the unity and interdependence of these opposites can preserve a sustainable
human society on our planet.
Amsterdam: Amsterdam University Press, 2002

Water: The Blood of the Earth.
Lack of access to clean and sufficient water in many parts of the world, especially
in Asia and Africa, will be a major issue in the coming decades. This book presents
an overall view on the diversity of problems and solutions, based on the author's
involvement in water-related projects. He also explores the human relationship
with water and the spiritual meanings we ascribe to it.
New York: Cosimo Books, 2007

Three Windows on Eternity: Exploring Evolution and Human Destiny.
With its compelling combination of science and spirituality, *Three Windows
on Eternity* offers an eye-opening way to understand the relationship between
consciousness and the universe beyond. Taking a very personal journey from
the Big Bang to the 21st century, Allerd Stikker offers a unique interpretation of
evolution, one that focuses on our inner perception and tries to restore coherence
and hope in a seemingly divided and disintegrating world.
London: Watkins Publishing, 2013

Other inspiring titles on faith and conservation by Bene Factum

FAITH IN FOOD
Changing the world—one meal at a time
Edited by Sue Campbell and Susie Weldon

"Never doubt that a small group of thoughtful, committed individuals can change the world, indeed it's the only thing that ever has."
—Margaret Mead, American cultural anthropologist.

The Alliance of Religions and Conservation (ARC) has come together with representatives of six of the world's major religions (Buddhism, Christianity, Hinduism, Islam, Judaism and Sikhism) to shine a light on how we deal with one of the most important parts of our lives—food. Eating is a moral act: our choices of what, when and how we eat have a huge impact upon the Earth, our fellow human beings and other living creatures.

Faith in Food is a unique vision, combining essays, scripture, story-telling, recipes, initiatives and general wisdom in this beautifully produced book, all seeking to challenge and explore our relationship with what we eat, and how we obtain our food.

In the foreword to *Faith in Food*, HRH Prince Charles, The Prince of Wales, says:

"The world is waking up to the fact that we have to find ways to produce food more sustainably because of the enormous challenges facing us. With accelerating climate change, rising costs of fuel and fertiliser and a rapidly growing global population, we need to ask whether the way we produce our food is fit for purpose in the very challenging circumstances of the 21st century. We simply cannot ignore that question any longer."

He concludes: "Our sacred traditions can lead us back into a 'right relationship' with the natural world and restore a sense of reverence for the food that sustains us, the creation that provides it and for the noble profession of farming, the very foundation of a healthy civilisation."

Paperback
ISBN: 978-1-909657-41-0
Price: £14.99

STORIES OF THE STRANGER
Encounters with exiles and outsiders
Collected by Martin Palmer and Katriana Hazell

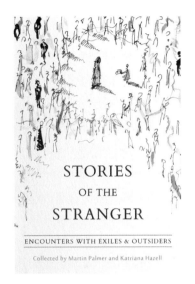

A selection of brilliant writers, young and old, have come together to retell some of the world's most culturally defining tales about encounters with strangers, with poignancy, humour and wit.

The experience of losing everything, of being thrown out, of being dispossessed, exiled and being forced to rely on the generosity (or not) of others, is a fundamental and recurring theme in many world cultures. Furthermore every major spiritual tradition tells stories of how you are more likely to meet the divine in the outcast, the beggar, or the stranger, than you are in the king, the queen, or indeed the priest.

Twenty short stories, sitting alongside raw and powerful illustrations, remind readers of the importance of strangers and what stands to be learned from engaging with them.

Paperback
ISBN: 978-1-909657-44-0
Price: £9.99

About ARC
The Alliance of Religions and Conservation (ARC) was founded in 1995 by HRH the Duke of Edinburgh. Its mission is to help major religions around the world develop and carry out their own individual environmental programmes, because—in different ways—their own core teachings, beliefs and practices all have nature at their core. ARC also works with key environmental organisations to help them link with religions, creating powerful alliances between faith communities and conservation groups.